Democratizing the Police

Recent Publications by the Author

- **Constitution of India: Vision, Reality, Reform**
  CPPSD, Hyderabad, 1998
- **Managing a Vision:** Democracy, Development & Governance
  Gyan, New Delhi, 2005.
- **Managing India:** Professionalization of Politics
  Forthcoming, 2013

Democratizing the Police

Indian Scenario

G.R.S. Rao

SHIPRA

ISBN: 978-81-7541-681-9

First Published in India in 2013

Democratizing the Police: Indian Scenario

SHIPRA PUBLICATIONS
H.O.: LG 18-19, Pankaj Central Market, Patparganj,
I.P. Ext., Delhi-110092, Tel: 91-11-2223 5152, 2223 6152
Br.Off.: 4617/18, Ansari Road, Darya Ganj,
New Delhi-110002, Tel: 6594 6453, 9810522367
E-mail: info@shiprapublications.com
www.shiprapublications.com

Dedicated to

Police in India
with a prayer for zero Loss of Life
in protecting and promoting
democracy, peace and harmony

Foreword

The public perception of the police in this country is unflattering. There is a deep-rooted and widely held suspicion bordering on hostility with regard to the intentions and operational methods of the police force. This is perhaps a hark back to the pre-independence days when it was widely felt that the police went beyond its normal functions of the maintenance of law and order and the prevention and investigation of crime to being used as a coercive instrument of the State to keep a watch on and suppress legitimate political nationalist activities. The fact that this view of the police is still held reflects both an inadequate appreciation by the general public of the legitimate role of police on the one hand and, the thinking and actions of the police force itself in the discharge of its functions. The fact that there is suspicion about the police force as an instrument of coercion, which is held even 60 years after independence and against the background of a vibrant pluralist democracy and, country of rich ethnic religious and cultural diversity, should be a matter of concern. Participants in the political process should obviously refrain from using the police to further their political agenda and partisan interests. An efficient, neutral and honest police force which would steer clear of partisan policies and not be tainted by political, caste and sectarian bias is what the Constitution enjoins and what the public expects from the police. It calls for both a liberal understanding by the general public of the legitimate functions of the police as much as reform within the police system to make it a relevant instrument in the maintenance of law and order in a liberal democracy against the background of a still evolving paradigm of the relations between the State and the Citizen. The police force is an important instrument in furthering our liberal democracy with its emphasis on the Rule of Law. This calls for internal reform to change the mindset of the political parties as much in the police to operate in and sustain democratic values and institutions.

This is an important subject and, in this book, Dr G R S Rao, a political sociologist and research scholar of eminence has analysed the interplay of various factors in the evolving saga of a liberal democracy facing multifarious challenges such as violent left wing extremism and sectarian strife and the role and functions of the police. This calls also for internal reform in the police to subserve larger national objectives. This book deals with these aspects and policies with emphasis on internal change and reform of the police system, tellingly encapsulated in the title of the book, Democratising the Police. It is an important work and makes a significant contribution to the ongoing debate on the role of the police.

8 March 2013 **M. Narasimham**
Hyderabad

Preface

As a student, I had chosen to study and explore the esoteric combination of law and sociology, with cultural anthropology as an adjunct. The focus was on theories and concepts. It was sheer 'divine' that I had the professional opportunity to continue my exploration, in my own chosen field through research, training, management development and consulting. It was a continuity, with a shift from the academic disciplinary pursuit, theoretical and conceptual, to the realm of addressing live social issues and problems, which warranted trans-disciplinary method and cross-cultural perspectives.

Sponsored research on communal conflict, caste conflict, industrial strife, regional and linguistic tensions, secular divide; consulting assignments in areas such as 'Policy Issues and Directions' on Left Wing Extremism (Government of AP), reorganization of Central Reserve Police Force (CRPF) Government of India (MHA); Committee work on Security Management for Prasar Bharati; as a Member of the National Committee on Police Training (BPR & D, MHA, Government of India); organizing a series of National Workshops on Public Policy Management for senior Indian Police Service (IPS), Indian Administrative Service (IAS) Officers and political executives (Ministers) belonging to the entire political spectrum (of INC, BJP, TDP, CPI (M), Shiv Sena, Akali Dal, Janata Dal, NCP et al) from all the states of India; alongside opportunities as a Guest Faculty or a Resource Person at several national academies and conferences covering aspects such as 'internal security', 'participative democracy', 'distortions of development', 'federal polity' and 'good governance' provided opportunities and proved a professional feast. Truly, these opportunities yielded unlimited dividends of professional enrichment.

Of equal, if not greater, significance are the informal, unstructured interactions spread over several months of working together with two esteemed friends from police organizations. They are-Shri Ganeshwar Jha, I.P.S. who held critical positions culminating as the Director of Sardar Vallabhbhai Patel National Police Academy; and Shri. George C. Francis, who proved to be an encyclopaedia of CRPF, who rose, with his 'dedication' to the rank of I.G. of Police at the Head Quarters. This expression is not, not at all, an 'acknowledgement', but grateful reflection of 'professional partnership' fructifying into personal friendship. This publication thus, represents an output of a series of creative interactions with a large number of persons who have rich experience on diverse concepts, contexts, experiments.

A nascent democracy, with rich as well as diverse and clashing ethnicities, caught in a long and continuing flare offers many a challenge as a part of and to the process of social transformation. The police forces face the greatest challenge of maintaining a modicum of dynamic equilibrium in the rapidly changing pluralist society, as to help maintain social harmony while promoting the process of dynamic development. Are the police 'expected' to promote stability as well as change? What are the perceptions of police, of their role in the 'social transformation' in the vibrant democracy of India? If there is a role, do the police have to redefine their role as a constant, in tune with the evolutionary change, and reengineer their 'organization', not merely in structural terms but also in ethical, cultural and processual terms?

These and many more similar and serious issues of concern emerge to the fore; there is nothing like a "right" or a "wrong" solution. This publication, it is hoped, which raises a series of issues, will promote a wider debate in the polity, leading to productive and democratic responses, thus tuning the police to a higher degree of role clarity, normative setting, and effectiveness as an organization contributing to its mission of national harmony and democratic transformation.

Brisbane, California **G.R.S. Rao**

Acknowledgements

Acharya is one who stimulates the creative power of thought, beyond imparting knowledge. This is all the more true where the teacher does not 'preach' standing on the high pedestal, but shares the thought process in the manner of sitting round the table, along with "participants" engaged in defining problems and exploring solutions, with a measure of professional conviction and social commitment. Participants in workshops are, as experienced or more experienced than the resource persons, who constitute as panels to bring out the multi-dimensional perspectives, issues and plausible solutions.

No wonder any series of national level workshops bring out the best of creative approaches and solutions to the management of public affairs. It is the leadership all the way - political, administrative, judicial, academic, media, who provide a 'think tank' mode of ambience, in the definition, exploration and analyses of social issues and an agenda of action.

The author had gained the best of professional insights while designing, developing, and organizing a series of national workshops. Such an opportunity yielded a rich harvest of data on various issues of concern to the nation. Two publications viz., *Constitution of India: Vision, Reality, Reform (1998), and, Managing A Vision: Democracy, Development, Governance* (2005); and this, the third crop emerged as *Democratizing the Police: The Indian Context* so far.

Thus, the author places on record his sense of gratitude to the participants, members of the multi-sectoral panels, and the two officers who were associated, nay involved, in the conduct of consulting assignments.

Shri. Ganeshwar Jha, IPS who was the Director of the SVP National Police Academy, and Shri. George C Francis, I.G. of Police CRPF, who teamed up along with the author to study the Mission Orientation of CRPF as an internal security organization. That 'team' of three continued with the spirit, reinforced beyond the assignment, worked through this publication. Shri. Ganeshwar Jha and Shri. George C Francis proved to be the 'mentors' to the author.

My sincere gratitude to Dr. S. Subramanian, IPS, who was the first Director of Special Police Group (SPG) who helped me to crystallize the title and theme of this publication; and to Shri. K. Vijaya Rama Rao, IPS, formerly Director of the Central Bureau of Investigation, and later a Minister in the Government of Andhra Pradesh State. He gave me so much time first to closely read through, and then the benefit of extended interaction on the draft. I am beholden to Dr. M. Narasimham, Chairman Emeritus, Court of Governors, Administrative Staff College of India for writing the 'Foreword' for the book. I thank Shipra Publications, Delhi, especially Shri D. Kumar for the professional quality of publication.

Shri. Prakash Walke, Librarian and Information Officer at the SVP National Police Academy helped me with some quantitative data. Smt. N. Suseela and Shri. N. Mohan of Sashi Services helped me with the several rounds of DTP work. P.V. Seshagiri Rao, a young professional with his critical mind and sharp eyes helped me in the editing of the zero draft.

Contents

List of Illustrations

1

State of Democracy: India at 60

Democracy by definition encompasses two facets, that of form and substance. Under ideal conditions, it is best described as 'a way of life'. What is 'alive' remains dynamic, leading to diverse mutations and evolving patterns. It is this dynamic character that lends the third dimension to democracy, the 'way of life', contributing to the kaleidoscopic view of democracy.

The dynamic character of democracy is manifest in a variety of range and patterns of political organization, with a mosaic of economic, social and cultural factors. Some of the predominant patterns labeled as kingdoms; some of the kings proclaiming themselves as the divine 'representatives', totalitarian 'peoples', liberal and capitalist *et al*. People do play a role as silent majorities and select activists, in shaping the diverse mutations and patterns of democracy, as has been witnessed through the prism of time and space. The village republics, represented yet another variant of 'socio-economic-political' organization carrying the brand label of 'direct' democracy, in contrast to 'representative' democracy. With trade and commerce (as it evolved during the 18th and 19th centuries) leading to 'colonialism', some of the early 'industrialized' countries built empires, through economic and military domination over half the world. This 'alien' rule has led to the alienation of the people, transforming them through 'democratic' awakening and assertion for political freedom. While many of such colonized countries had adopted aggressive and violent eruptions and 'won' political freedom, India had evolved a mode of popular movement', as a mutant of 'war without violence' and nourished the 'liberal' spirit of democracy. Indian quest and movement for freedom was chiselled by its own native genius. It was also inspired by the American War of Independence and the French Revolution, two main streams of freedom and democracy in contemporary history. In the clutch of such historical factors, India's attainment of democracy and freedom shaped its image as the 'Light of Asia', and as a 'role model' of the democratic wave that swept, especially, the Asian and African continents.

Liberal democracy emerged as the mainstream 'ideal' of the people under alien subjugation all over the globe. The leadership of the freedom movement in India was 'intellectual' as much as it was 'political' and they both blended in shaping its character, substance and modus. The democratic freedom movement evolved and revolved around ideals such as responsibility, tolerance, social justice, equal opportunity, and pluralism, based on active, equal and participatory citizenship at all levels. In the spectrum of Indian diversity, the spirit of liberal democracy has remained multi-dimensional leading to shades or shapes both at the centre and the periphery; it has represented a confluence of collective identities.

Vision and Mission of the Republic

The Constituent Assembly (consembly, in short) was constituted in 1948, comprising 348 members, elected by the provincial legislative assemblies that were set up and operating on the basis of elections that were held in 1945. The then Congress party had an overwhelming majority in all the provinces and consequently, in the Constituent Assembly. However, the national leadership of the Indian National Congress (Congress Party, in short) assured itself that persons with exceptional abilities and an image of high integrity found place in the Consembly. Representation of the minority communities was also ensured.

Members of the Consembly were elected not on the basis of adult suffrage, which was to come later as a result of the Constitution. The Indian National Congress set up its own candidates as well as many non-Congress candidates, such as B.R. Ambedkar who were trenchant critics of the Congress. Ambedkar's name was suggested by no less a person than Gandhiji with whom

Ambedkar was never in agreement. K.M. Munshi was a member of the Congress Party, but had left it. Sir Alladi Krishnaswami, Sir N. Gopalaswami Ayyangar and several others were not even participants in any of the mass political movements, but were part of the Constituent Assembly. Sir Tej Bahadur Sapru was invited but his health did not permit him to join it. B.N. Rau was not a member of the Consembly but appointed as Constitutional Advisor.

India had a historical tradition of democracy, 'people-focussed' liberal administration even under kings and kingdoms. Thus, in a manner it was a democratic renaissance. This spirit was reflected even in the composition of the Consembly as a kaleidoscopic picture of India. It reflected youthful fervour as well as rich experience and diversity. Rich in educational background and professions, the Consembly reflected a wide spectrum of opinion that enriched the debates and deliberations. Most significant of all, India evolved as a consensual democracy.

The idea was not to fill the Assembly with only supporters of the mainstream Congress Party, but to get the stalwarts and best brains in the country. This fact has been emphasized by all the 43 surviving Members of the Consembly.[1] Recapitulating the days of formation of the Constituent Assembly, C. Subramaniam (CS), reminisces how the members of the assembly were selected from the respective provincial assemblies. Though the Congress Party was in a dominant position, it was determined to select persons of outstanding merit and distinction, particularly in law and public affairs. They also wanted the highest level of intellect and experience selected from all over the country so that they would represent all shades of opinion and all regions. C.S. illustrates the point by mentioning the names of Sir Alladi Krishnaswami who was a well known jurist, and of Dr. Jerome D'Souza a distinguished educationist.

Jawaharlal Nehru made a remarkable observation, in the Consembly, which was fully in tune with the occasion. He said: "Freedom and power bring responsibility. That responsibility rests upon this assembly, a sovereign body representing the sovereign people of India. Before the birth of freedom we have endured all the pains of labour and our hearts are heavy with the memory of this sorrow. Some of those pains continue even now. Nevertheless, the past is over and it is the future that beckons to us now." He continued: "That future is not one of ease or resting but of incessant striving so that we might fulfill the pledges we have so often taken and the one we shall take today. The service of India means the service of the millions who suffer. It means the ending of poverty and ignorance and disease and inequality of opportunity. The ambition of the greatest man of our generation has been to wipe every tear from every eye. That may be beyond us; but as long as there are tears and suffering, so long our work will not be over[2]." Democracy in India had not emerged as a static mould, but was conceived and evolved as a futuristic, dynamic charter of change with a direction and destiny.

In the Indian context, politics (institutions and processes) were perceived and pursued as the prime mover of democracy, and political process as the process of social engineering, tempering a traditional society into a liberal democracy.

Social revolution, in an evolutionary mode, was the most important of many of the goals the Constitution framers had in mind. They envisioned that only through social transformation the basic needs of the common man could be fulfilled, translating the vision of free India into a reality. Along with social revolution, the goals of national unity and stability had also predominated the minds of members of the Consembly. Interests of minority communities, efficient administration and national security, were certain other aims which influenced the shaping of the Constitution. The Constitution was predominantly "a product of the social content of the independence movement, which in turn stemmed from an awareness of the plight of the mass of Indians, so the practical provisions were largely a product of the Assembly members' experience in government and of the exigencies of the times".[3]

Reflecting on the Objectives Resolution, Alladi Krishnaswami stated that "the main object of this Assembly is . . . . to give concrete expression to the surging aspirations of a people yearning for freedom by framing a constitution for a free and independent India, for the good of the people, one and all, of this great and historic land, irrespective of caste, class, community or creed, with a hoary civilization going back to several centuries".[4]

In an age of revolutions—political, economic and social—Jawaharlal Nehru was emphatic that India would inevitably be a Republic. "Now, some friends have raised the question: Why have you not put in the word 'democratic' here? Well, I told them that it is conceivable, of course, that a republic may not be democratic but the whole of our past is witness to this fact that we stand for democratic institutions".[5]

> WHEREIN all power and authority of the Sovereign Independent India, its constituent parts and organs of government, are derived from the people; and
>
> WHEREIN shall be guaranteed and secured to all the people of India justice, social, economic and political: equality of status, of opportunity, and before the law: freedom of thought, expression, belief, faith, worship, vocation, association and action, subject to law and public morality: and
>
> WHEREIN adequate safeguards shall be provided for minorities, backward and tribal areas, and depressed and other backward classes; and
>
> WHEREBY shall be maintained the integrity of the territory of the Republic and its sovereign rights of land, sea, and air according to justice and the law of civilized nations, and
>
> This ancient land attains its rightful and honoured place in the world and make its full and willing contribution to the promotion of world peace and the welfare of mankind.

During the consembly debates, Dr. Ambedkar commented thus: "Whoever captures power will not be free to do what he likes with it. In the exercise of it, he will have to respect these .... Directive Principles. He cannot ignore them. He may not have to answer for their breach in a Court of Law. But he will certainly have to answer for them before the electorate at election time. What great value these Directive Principles possess will be realized better when the forces of right contrive to capture power".[6] Ananthasayanam Iyengar emphasized that if this Constitution is worked in the spirit in which it has been framed, I am sure we will be one of the foremost nations of the world."[7]

India's freedom movement started with an 'awakening' of the people to the historical distortions, extant realities, and to the futuristic hopes, aspirations and challenges. Any movement, in order to be successful, needs a leadership with a vision and commitment to a set of ideals and goals. It is impossible to recapture, in isolation, the nature and quality of leadership that proved to be the singular strength of India's freedom movement. Suffice it to say that the leadership was inseparable from the movement, its ideological currents, and modes of thought and action.

Reflecting on leadership it may be relevant to recall as to what Mohammed Ali Jinnah, the self-proclaimed protector of the interests of the Indian Muslims had to say, about the Muslims that would be left behind in India, after partition. To quote M.C. Chagla: "It is absurd to think of a house for the Muslims, when as many as 60 million Muslims were left behind in India. I remember once asking Jinnah: you are fighting for Pakistan mainly in the interest of the Muslim-majority states. But what happens to the Muslims in the States particularly like Uttar Pradesh where they are in small minority? I will never forget the answer Jinnah gave me. He looked at me for a while and said: "They will look after themselves. I am not interested in their fate".[8] Indian tradition of democracy had evolved as a pluralistic and secular polity, thanks to the vision of its leadership.

India woke up to "life and freedom" on the midnight of August 14, 1947. The saga of a long struggle and sacrifices of the thousands of patriots ended and India attained her rightful place in the world as an independent nation ready to accept the challenge of shaping its destiny. One of the early challenges independent India had to face was the one posed by the princely states. Some of the princes desired complete independence, a course which, the government of the Indian Union declared, "threatened to bespatter the country with a vast number of independent enclaves, large and small, an eventuality which if not prevented. . . . could have wrecked the economy of the country, broken its unity as a nation, menaced its security every moment of its existence, vitiated its resurgent democratic spirit and brought about balkanization whose effects would be irreparable". This daunting task of integrating the 500 odd princely states fell on the shoulders of Sardar Vallabhbhai Patel, a stalwart and a statesman *par excellence* who has rightly been called "the Bismarck of India" and even more appropriately the 'Iron Man' of free India. Through his persuasive power, diplomatic skill, political adroitness he was able to bring about the administrative unity and integration of this vast country, which is the essential base for building up a strong democratic nation. By integrating 500 plus states and the elimination of centuries-old autocracies, Indian democracy registered a historic achievement in the annals of history.

The birth of India as an independent country had brought about a sea change in the situation that obtained during the century of freedom struggle the world over. The role and process of governance itself had been transformed from one of maintaining *status quo* to that of bringing about social transformation, *Samaj Parivartan* the cardinal objective of the freedom movement. "The soul of our constitution is the prescription of human rights and dignity of citizens in the broadest sense of these expressions, on a continuing basis",[9] observed K.R. Virulkar in the Constituent Assembly.

Social transformation was the most important of the many goals the constitution framers had in mind. Along with social revolution, the goals of national unity, integrity and stability had also predominated the minds of members of the Consembly. Interests of minority communities, efficient administration and national security, constituted the aims which influenced the shaping of the Constitution.

Politics: The Prime Mover

Political power, appropriated by the British, was wrested back by the people of India through the popular freedom movement. Democracy was the mode adopted by the 'demos', the people of India, to channelize this political power as the 'prime mover' of the country, and its transformation into a nation. Democratization involved translation of the vision into a reality, shaping the political, economic, social and cultural ground conditions of the Indian society.

During the two historical phases of the freedom movement, and of sculpting the constitution as the vision document of India, political processes had channelized the energies of the various sections of society towards the devolution of political power within the framework of a democratic ethic. Politicization was focused on mainstreaming the people leading to their 'organization' and participation in the struggle for freedom. Until India attained Independence, 'freedom' meant awareness and 'empowerment'. It got expanded and transformed thereafter, into options, alternative paths, such as decentralization, participation and a measure of responsible citizenship matching a responsive administration.

Politics as the prime mover sets out any society on the path of social change, *Samaj Parivartan*. Politics constituted an onerous role and responsibility of promoting a 'democratic' dialogue and debate on the options, choices and even more critically, promoting harmonization of the possible conflict of the diverse values, identities and interests of the people, in a pluralist society. Democracy promotes and sustains credibility and legitimacy of the institutions of politics viz. political parties, and processes such as election of representatives. It will remain credible and legitimate as long as the processes of awareness and empowerment of people are promoted and the diverse social conflicts are harmonized.

'Politicization' of issues is the vital process, the prerequisite, for political process to perform its role as the prime-mover of a society, especially in a democracy. However, when politics and politicization shift their concern from the Gandhian premise of 'people' – orientation to the Weberian postulate of 'power', this process of democratic 'social transformation' gets distorted; the process turns malignant by generating and accentuating conflict in place of harmony. When the political process turns malignant, social transformation gets distorted; democratic polity itself gets exposed to the malignancies. Loss of legitimacy leads to and gets reflected in diverse manifestations of conflict, violence and a slide in rule of law, the touchstone of democratic order.

Several vital issues and aspects of the nature of political process emerge for consideration in any discussion on the impact of the character of political process on the democratic quality of Indian polity. The first prerequisite of a democratic polity is to place the people at the centre of the process as a constant, to map the potential impact of democratic transformation and to measure its impact on peoples. In the Indian context, as the political process has turned partisan and malignant, it had its impact on the quality of its democratic status and process. Disgruntled 'dissidents' within a political party 'generating' anti-reservation, communal, caste, regional, linguistic as well as class-conflicts and mass-scale violence to run down its own leadership, reflects the nature and degree of loss of democratic ethic within the party, polity and society. Issues of extremism were not deliberated within the legislatures, but such conflicts were constantly used and abused as a part of the rhetoric as between 'ruling' and 'opposition' 'national' and 'regional' political parties. Undeclared 'electoral' understandings between political parties and 'extremists', and reversal of policy declarations and dispositions both before and after elections have not only changed political fortunes, but also aggravated the pre-existing conflicts and triggered fresh conflicts, political as well as social.

Claims are ignited for 'autonomy' among regional, ethnic groups in the form of (a) autonomous councils, (b) centrally administered regions, and (c) small states in order to gain partisan political advantage with disastrous consequences to the people and to the nation as a whole. Indulging in a blame-game merely in order to derive partisan-political advantage, within a debased framework of secularism and communalism, merely to build up 'vote-banks' without ever attempting to operationalize the concept of secularism, has become a 'constant' in turning the democratic Indian politics malignant. Judicial intervention and direction to correct such distortions have had no positive impact on such distortions.

Setting up 'high-level' and 'high-power committees, or commissions (with sitting Judges, either of the Supreme Court or of High Courts, and more often with retired Judges, left the citizens wondering as to what exactly makes a commission 'judicial');

appointment of 'advisors' by the administrative ministries to produce overnight reports without any basis or support of empirical data; securing the seal of an 'expert' on the dotted lines where there are statutory commissions such as the Backward Classes Commission, have emerged as the institutional mechanisms devised by the political process merely to gain political mileage at the expense of democratic legitimacy. The appointment of (retired) Justice Banerjee by the Ministry of Railways and another Judicial Commission by the Government of Gujarat to inquire into the (2002) Godhra train fire, both the reports of Judicial Commissions ending up in the Supreme Court, reveal instances of partisan political drama even in the face of social trauma.

The partisan 'malignant' process of politics has been, vividly revealed in the attempted review of the Constitution of India where administrative orders were issued without a resolution of the parliament setting up of a National Commission. Even more curious, the terms of reference were tailored to meet the demands of the chairman leading to exclusion from the proposed review, some of the critical and politically controversial provisions of the constitution. The National Commission, so constituted, had negated itself; the partisan political process had deprived the nation of a much needed review of the Constitution.[10]

Such distortions were reflected even when eminent Jurists, (such as the Sachchar Committee), conditioned by the partisan political process, were denounced by a Muslim woman who observed that "Muslim means not only men, but also women. Appeasement is the name of the game that the political parties play without any rules or umpiring." The frequent clashes, communal, caste, regional, language *et al* as a threat to democracy in India, have emerged from the abandonment of civilized debate, and the adoption of violent means. Schism, conflict and violence, have emerged as the mode of political parties in the management of democracy in India. Ethnic cleansing, traumatic changes effected in the demographic profiles, massive scale of refugees of development, and illegal migrants from across the national boundaries have impacted the character of pluralism as a corner stone of Indian democracy.

Nationalism has not only not been promoted, but has been on a rapid slide, right from 1950; people have not inculcated citizenship, and pride of Indian citizenship. The process of acquiring power at any cost, and retaining at "all costs" has generated internal conflict in a manner and to an extent where strife and violence have fractured the Indian polity. An injury to the body when left untreated, attracts 'external/factors that infect the body politic.

There is a high degree of recklessness in the dispositions of political parties, engrossed in the creation of 'vote-banks'. They have not taken cognizance of the observations and directions of the Supreme Court, while dismissing a petition challenging an Orissa law that required police verification of all religious conversions. The Supreme Court, *inter alia,* had observed on Article 25(1) of the Constitution: "The Article postulates that there is no fundamental right to convert another person to one's own religion because if a person purposely undertakes the conversion of another person to his religion, that would impinge on the freedom of conscience guaranteed to all the citizens of the country."[11]

Human society, in its quest for enhanced quality of life had carved out visions of hopes, measured in centennial time-frames, of universal progression. During the 19th century, industrialization was perceived as the harbinger of hope and prosperity but ended up with the most exploitative socio-economic conditions and 'organized' conflict. 20th Century has spurred economic growth measured in terms of Gross Domestic Product (GDP) as the indicator of development, to only make large sections of people experience, all over the world, massive deterioration in the quality of life. Human Development Index (HDI) has revealed the rich getting richer subsidized by the poor. The Global Dialogue on Development (1990-2000) has brought out the need for democratic decentralization, and people's participation and empowerment as the *sine qua non* for 'inclusive' 'people-centric' development. Here again, the global society perceived that in fact, it is heading towards more 'authoritarian' regimes, externally induced regime changes, centralized bureaucracies, and political recentralization leaving the people alienated, hostile and subjugated. The twentieth century has also seen technological advances, but accompanied by subjugation of the human spirit, and leading to accentuated, disastrous management of people by the people. India has not proved an exception to these 'contra-indicators' of democracy.

The disastrous management, especially by the 'power-centric' political and administrative leadership is leading to an ever-deepening divide instead of a shared vision of democracy and the spirit of nationalism. If some nation states have emerged as 'failed' states, social strife is expanding and intensifying in states striving to promote democracy. If the macro scenario is characterized by fear, extremism and terrorism, the micro view is characterized by violent agitational methods, and a non-responsive civic-governance, fiscal corruption leading to corrosion of the system of governance and an alarming rise in phenomena such as farmers' suicides.

An anarchic condition, even if it is called 'functional', as Indian democracy has been taunted, is the consequence of a clash between the popular urges that are aroused in a liberal democracy, and a control exercised by feudalistic forces and vested interest groups in their attempt to wrest and retain "power" by all means mostly foul. In India's faulted democratic polity, the means vis-à-vis ends debate continues. Rule of law ceases to be of critical significance where laws do not remain a means, but acquire the character of rule by a coterie of individuals as an end in itself.

Economic stagnation and a slide in HDI have led to severe distortions in democracies leading to a rise in social turbulence with the consequence of autocracies or dictatorships in many a developing democracy during the 1980s. The situation threw up dictators who in course of time touted themselves as the champions of 'democratic' social agenda, and 'democratic' elections.
Electoral systems, the very basic process of democratic power, had not attained a stable state even after six decades of political freedom. As a part of the process of power even the Judicial institutions have been dragged into the street battles of 'power struggle'. The situation is tending to prove congenial for fundamentalism and terrorism to dominate and traumatize the democracies, and their sovereign status. When democracy, i.e. democratically elected government fails to narrow the social divide,

it tends to get destabilized by the resultant discord, crime, violence and institutionalized corruption. The end consequence is state terrorism, and rogue states start ruling the people.

Democracy in India, which had generated expectations on a global scale, as a 'role model', and as the 'Light of Asia', has witnessed the process of what has come to be called politicization of crime and criminalization of politics with the consequences of (a) political turmoil, (b) social fragmentation, and (c) a fractured polity. There was a threat of a meltdown of the democratic system in India. If the rules of the game constitute the life-line of democracy, the all-pervasive violence and power processes had dented, if not destroyed, the character of democracy in India. As a nation, India seems to be at war with itself, with debating electoral reform, all the time attaining a higher decibel. The agenda has remained and has grown critical; an ideal setting inviting external forces of destabilization. India is in urgent need of a surgical electoral reform to save its democratic character. When the *Majhi* the boatsman threatens the safety of the boat midstream, who can save the passengers? In India, the invariable demand is on the availability of police battalions to contain electoral fraud, turbulence, and violence in order to save democracy.

Progression of Democracy: Regression of Governance: The Indian Paradox

The institutional structures of governance have bulged in size, proliferated like the prop 'roots' of a banyan tree and yet in India's democracy there is a (quantitatively as well as qualitatively) growing hiatus and hostility between the demos and the units and branches of state. Governance process itself is degenerating, primarily because of corruption of functionaries and consequent corrosion of the 'steel frame' as the institutions of governance were being referred to.

The political parties and consequently the legislative institutions have become so dysfunctional that instead of these institutions addressing their legitimate responsibilities of resolving peoples' problems, people are left with resolving the deadlocks in the working of these institutions. It is not just monetary corruption, but they are enveloped by a spectrum of criminalization of politics, physical violence breaking out in the legislatures (and the national parliament), warranting the 'law of the Marshals'. At the advent of the 21st century democracy in India can be stated to be moving towards a polity where citizens are left in the lurch without representatives.

Public servants strike Indian democracy with a deadly certainty just before the democratic elections – threatening to convert the 'festival' of democracy into a funeral of the Republic. Corrupt political parties do not have the moral stamina and conviction to discipline 'public servants'. Any attempt, on the part of higher judiciary *suo motu* or, as a part of public interest litigation (PIL) or, under the provisions of the Essential Services Maintenance Act, to prohibit lightning 'strikes' and *bandhs* is loudly protested and public property destroyed as if it is a Fundamental Right. Even sabotage, disruption of public order, and murders, are condoned under pressure, at huge cost to the public and, indeed, at the cost of democratic order. The public is reduced to the status of servants of government functionaries, paying the penalty of increasing costs for a constantly deteriorating quality of governance.

State governments indulge in assaulting the process of Rule of Law – the foundations of our constitutional democracy – through measures such as '*Salwa Judum*' (arming the people to fight left wing extremists), setting up exclusive battalions of tribal youth, and ill-conceived proportions, such as 'minority' police *et al.*

The hundred years (1857-1947) of freedom movement described as a war without violence had promoted the spirit of nationalism and a vision of development as reflected in the Constitution of India, and the consensual mode adopted in formulating it. But, during the first six decades after freedom, Indian society has moved on the path of social fragmentation, and into a fractured society, a country fighting itself. Gandhi, hailed as the 'Father of the Nation' summarized succinctly.

So far we are going downhill, on the path of progress. If India continues to be a democracy, the credit goes to the people who sustained democracy, trying to provide correctives all the time. Do the police in India truly represent that ethos, remaining loyal to the Constitution and accountable to the demos? If the power process grows strongly as the preoccupation of our political parties, India may soon witness the need for setting up a police outpost in the national and state legislatures. Can such a situation be described as police *Raj*?

The gap between the vision and reality can make all the difference as between social integration and harmony on the one hand, and fragmentation and disintegration on the other. If the 20th century had witnessed what can be described as unity to fight colonial exploitation, 21st century phenomena of development is showing signs of an emerging pattern of conflicts that could challenge national integrity and integration as projected in Illustration 1

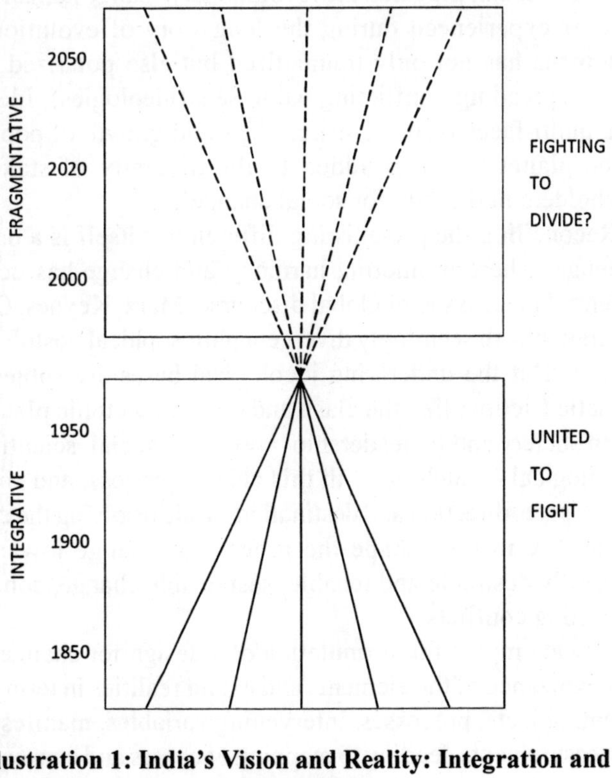

Illustration 1: India's Vision and Reality: Integration and Fragmentation

With the emergence of a liberalized era of globalization (and democratization *et. al*) and the institutions of global governance, political and economic factors have fused into a bloody mix of criminalization on a global scale that the national governments are left to grapple with. Communities around the world appear to be heading towards what Samuel P. Huntington had observed (*Foreign Affairs* Summer 1993) that the fundamental source of conflict in the emerging world will not be primarily ideological or economic but cultural, the fault lines between civilizations will be the battle lines of the future. Emerging democracies have to learn to deal with this whirlpool of culture conflict.

Political freedom, liberal democracy, industrial revolution and economic liberalization, together constitute the most powerful phenomenon that triggered the revolutionary change human society had ever experienced during the long story of evolution. This phenomena has not only traumatized but also polarized human society, spreading conflicting value sets (ideologies), identities, and a multi-faceted social strife. The rapid growth of population on the planet has also added to the diversity of stakes and stakeholders in the 'run for social change'.

Reconciling the pre-existing differentials itself is a daunting challenge, where promoting harmony and change has occupied the central place issue of global discourse. Marx, Keynes, Gandhi, *et al* argued with seemingly divergent philosophical postulates and postures. But the underlying ideological bases are subjected to traumatic friction, like the clash and crash of tectonic plates. Can human society and its leadership – political, social, scientific and technological – catch up with this change process, and shape its context, pace, direction and destination, while resolving the existing conflicts? Can they shape the process of change towards the universally desirable and tenable, sustainable change, containing the existing conflicts?

Any attempt at the formulation of a design for change has to take cognizance of the elements and extant realities in terms of the content, objects, processes, intervening variables, manifestations and measurements, leading to mapping of causes and consequences in their cyclical network of relationships; the intended as well as the unintended. Access to and control (ownership) over land, water, energy and environment, emerge as the core issues of contention, demanding synchronization both at the individual (micro) as well as collective (macro) levels. These vital resources, scarce as they are, have to be protected and shared equitably, so as to ensure sustainability.

In the Indian context, the phenomena of industrial revolution, urbanization *et al* right from (a) Rourkela [1950s] to Nandigram, (2009) (b) Nagarjuna Sagar [1950s] to Narmada Dam (2000), in almost all the spheres of planned development, the process of economic growth has been always and almost uniformly, guided by the economic growth indicators to the exclusion of any serious consideration of what and how 'growth' matters to human development, leading to consequences such as massive alienation and hostility. The process of growth had generated and reflected 'exploitative' practices, neglect of employment, accentuation of regional imbalances – manifested as ethnic conflict, linguistic and regional tensions (locals vs. outsiders, sons of the soil), and homelessness. We are still debating issues with pseudo labels such as Naxalism. The 'undemocratic' methods of both peoples and governments labeled variously as 'extremism', 'state terrorism, 'guns vs. butter' and 'rogue leadership' *et al* are pitted against the democratic mode.

Factors and manifestations may be many but all of them together, like tributaries of a mighty river, contribute to the Gross Social Conflict (GSC) in India. If social conflict is not managed adequately, appropriately and in good time, it can become the singlemost man-made disaster, devastating the democratic character of India. A failure on this front can make a case study on 'disastrous management'. It is not a static law and order that the police have to manage. It is the turbulence as a consequence of the dynamic processes of social engineering and social transformation.

Gross Social Conflict

An overview of six decades of planned development reveals that India has attained great economic heights (though not matching its endowment of natural and human resources), but in the process has lost its 'social sights', the end objectives of 'economic growth' set around quality of life, which in the Indian ethos, as well as in the constitutional vision represents '*Pragati*' '*Abhyudaya*'. Planned development was projected in Rupees (crores) of budgetary allocations and economic growth measured in terms of GDP. There have emerged a series of fallacies, false assumptions and gross distortions – all of them having an adverse impact on sustainable development on the one hand and sustainability of democratic development on the other. As we have not succeeded in integrating democracy and development, we are witness to, as well as victims of democratically unsustainable levels of social conflict. We had assumed that development of backward areas would automatically lead to development of 'people' in backward areas, but have been proved miserably wrong by phenomena such as 'uncontrolled' mass migration of people endowed with "superior" knowledge and skills into underdeveloped areas, and large-scale projects located in backward areas with the consequence of mass displacement and distress migration of the 'local', 'rural', 'poor" and the 'tribal' communities driven to suffer life in urban slums. This has directly contributed to massive build-up of alienation, social disruption, conflict and recurring violence. Even in regard to access to community resources and basic necessities of life such as drinking water, the process of development has bypassed the poorer sections of communities. Their lands are alienated, rehabilitation in its qualitative dimensions viz., residential, occupational and socio-cultural, was not even appreciated much less attempted. In many cases whole villages have been bulldozed. For their drinking water needs they have to tread long distances, and be satisfied with water that doesn't quench their thirst but will bestow all sorts of diseases, leading to the dance of death. Even in urban areas, where drinking water sources are piped and distributed, statistics reveal a gross addition of water supply. What the statistics conceal is the fact that the rich get and use an abundance of filtered water (even for the toilets, gardens and swimming pools) while the *Bastis* get drinking water mixed up with sewerage matter. If it is the feudal pocket of Bihar, the rich maintain private armies as a tool for protecting themselves against the poor, often mocking the state while indulging in vengeful and brutal killing of the poor.

While discussing human development, issues of equity, such as 'financial affordability' versus 'availability and accessibility' for all; and creation of infrastructure at 'what cost' versus at 'whose (social) cost' become relevant but hardly considered. When development gets distorted through such processes as reverse subsidies, and issues are coloured or get clouded, hostile social relations lead to the emergence of phenomena such as 'Naxalism'. When the gaps between the pattern of economic growth (GDP) and Social Development (HDI) lead to an inverse ratio, or when social development lags far behind growth, such phenomenon leads to the consequence of Gross Social Conflict (GSC) as projected in Illustration 2. Democracy takes a dent and becomes vulnerable.

'Reservations' were conceived as a measure to gradually reduce disparities and thus move towards equalization of opportunities. But, the methods and manner of managing reservations by the political parties caught in the competitive bidding for power, suffice to say, the polity has been '*Mandalised*' – more appropriate expressions would be 'vandalisation'.

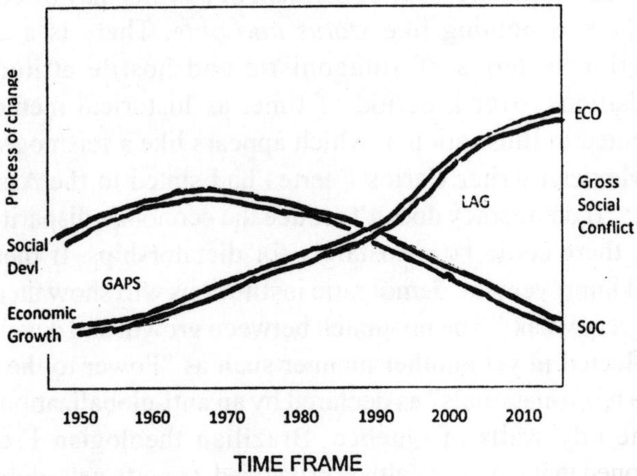

Illustration 2: Gross Social Conflict: Pattern of Gaps and Lags in the Process of Change

Instead of moving towards an egalitarian society without caste, we have moved from about 100 castes in 1950, to more than 4,000 castes by the year 2000; and, more and more 'castes' are agitating for labels of backward status. The same is true of what has come to be called pseudo secularism. One of the quintessential characteristics of a truly democratic society is secularism; if a society is not 'secular' it cannot qualify as a democracy. Yet, instead of promoting integration, nationalism and a culture of tolerance, political wisdom or expediency thought it appropriate, after a quarter century of constitutional democracy, to amend the Preamble to the Constitution in order to incorporate the expression 'secular' as a basic feature of democracy in India. Indian leadership believed in 'declaratory democracy' rather than working to promote a 'functional democracy'. This declaratory democracy has proved a fertile ground for the growth of intolerance, in myriad forms, for the growth and accretion of social conflict, which is a negation of liberal constitutional democracy. The country is more communal today than at the starting line. Worse, anyone can create a spark in society, and can affix the labels of 'caste' or 'communal' or any label. Caste, communal, ethnic, regional *et al* conflicts do not represent mere dots on the map of India in a time series. The flare emanating from any issue or incident of conflict may be contained but there is nothing like *status quo ante*. There is a constant accretion in terms of antagonistic and hostile attitudes and dispositions, over a period of time, as historical memories as presented in Illustration 3, which appears like a seismograph.

Mexican writer Carlos Fuertes had stated to the Associated Press: "If democracy doesn't reduce the economic disparities very soon, there could be a nostalgia for dictatorships. If there is no social improvement, democratic institutions will show themselves to be very weak." The mismatch between growth and development is reflected in yet another manner such as "Power to the people, not to multi-nationals" as declared by an anti-globalization graffiti on the city walls of Quebec. Brazilian theologian Frei Betto cautioned that when "wealth is privatized, poverty gets globalized".

Indian society today has yet to make a start on the path of creating a shared sense of, and pride in, citizenship, where citizens

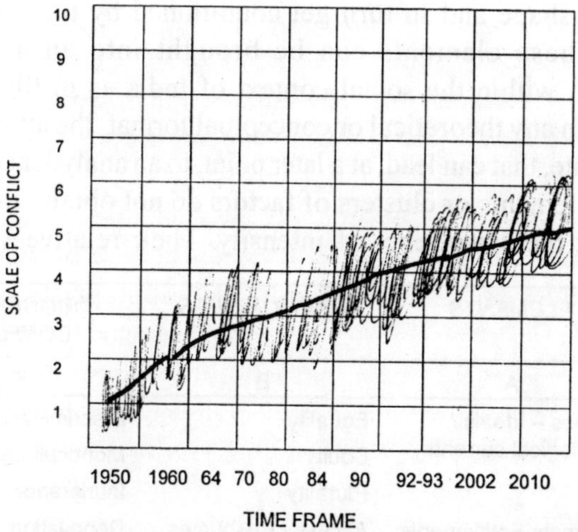

Illustration 3: Net Accretion of Social Conflict

together make a nation. India is today reduced to a geographical entity where a large number of 'minorities' (religious, caste, linguistic, ethnic, gender et al) make an alienated aggregation. If there are some 'citizens' they constitute a hapless minority. Long standing and constantly growing social conflict cannot sustain a democracy. When the prime movers of the polity i.e. the political parties and leaders operate on the premise of 'conflict' as the mode of securing and sustaining 'power' there emerge serious challenges before "we the people" who crave to make a nation. The processes of liberalization and globalization have only accentuated the Gross Social Conflict in India.

Analytically, basic elements of conflict in any society can be identified as falling into: (a) values, forming an ideological spectrum, (b) interests, clustering into social groups and classes, and (c) identities, that make enduring segmentation and fragmentation of a society. These basic elements or factors of conflict may operate either in isolation or in a mosaic of mutating patterns. This is where two other sets of factors emerge as the basic elements of conflict. These factors emerge from two social processes viz., (d) social change as a normal phenomenon obtaining in all societies, all the time, and (e) the institutions operating, seeking to shape and in turn get conditioned by the process of change. These elements can be brought into an analytical framework, within the social context of India as in Illustration. Instead of in any theoretical or conceptual format, the attempt here is to illustrate, that can lead, at a later point, to an analytical exercise. All these elements or clusters of factors do not obtain, much less operate, at the same level of intensity. Their relative values or

Sl. No.	*ELEMENTS*	*HARMONISERS*	*TRIGGERS OF CONFLICT*
	A	B	C
1	Values – Ideals / ideological currents	Equality Equity Plurality	Discrimination Monoculture Intolerance
2	Interests Entitlements	Access / Resources Water / Education Health / Justice Choice / Livelihoods	Deprivation Displacement Exploitation Marginalization Child labour
3	Identities	Pluralism Secularism Egalitarianism	Communalism Minoritism Reservation
4	Power	Democracy / Fair elections Freedom Liberty	Autocracy Feudalism Electoral Fraud
5	Social-Change GDP-HDI-GSC Historical Hangovers Quality of Life	Equalization of Development Equitable Development Reservations – Effective & time bound	Growing Disparities Social Distances / Prejudices Backlash Hostility Mandalization Distortions of Development
6	Complementary roles of Institutions of State	Shared Vision Common Objectives	Role-Goal conflict 'Power', 'Hierarchial' Orientations
7	Internal Security National integrity	Discipline of Democracy National Integration	Fundamentalism Extremism Mass Violence

Illustration 4: Elements and Triggers of Conflict in a Democratic Society

intensity depends upon the nature and degree of cognition, popular perceptions, enduring (hostile) attitudes, and behavioural dispositions apart from socio-economic and the 'environmental' triggers. Even more fascinating, for an analyst, they interact and impact in a situation-specific dynamic mode. The spectrum of these elements can be mapped out as a basis for bench-marking, measurement and to formulate strategies to manage conflict.

The polyglot society that is India, characterized by continental size, racial milieu, ethnic variety, cultural diversity, linguistic multiplicity, religious plurality, rural-urban hiatus not to speak of wide variations in the socio-cultural status of people based on age, gender and historical factors such as feudalism, mutations of caste and economic disparities, had secured political freedom at a great cost and effort, and gave unto itself a Constitution providing not merely the instrumentalities of governance, but also the goals of political, economic, social and cultural freedom as the agenda for social transformation — all this through a process of political consensualism which has itself been a unique feature of India's freedom movement. A design for change of a 'revolutionary order' in an 'evolutionary mode' – has been sculpted in the form of the Constitution, as a prescription for harmony and development. But an overview of the process of democratic transformation indicates that while nobody can make a serious issue of the pace of change in the face of the backlog, the direction, substance and the process of change have thrown up a wide range of negative indicators – 'triggers of conflict and a dilution of the harmonizers of democratic transformation. The several deficiencies in the democratic process of power are reflected in the emerging demand for 'None of The Above', NOTA, as a voting option. In the contemporary context, the political phenomena that can be labeled as '*Biharization*' has intensified conflict in the society. The emergence of 'anti-democratic' forces reflects the trigger effect of conflict that could be summed up in terms of 'Bullet for Ballot'. At a different level, it has assumed the proportions of 'cash for vote' in the innermost sanctum sanctorum of democracy viz., the parliament. India has registered a Gross Domestic Product based growth – but with two built-in contradictions. First, it is not 'inclusive' growth; second, pools of money based on "illegal activities including corruption, fraud, extortion and tax evasion", has emerged as a serious challenge to political (legitimate) authority, which unless the political system fights back, its backlash will destroy democracy.

Democracy means decentralization of power, people's participation (beyond casting a vote) and inclusiveness, rights of citizenship, empowerment and entitlements. Factors such as deprivation (of education, healthcare, livelihoods), exploitation (child labour, bonded labour), lack of access to water, to justice, and the rights of citizenship (which represent the core of human rights) have created a trigger effect on the nature and degree of social conflict. Who is exploiting whom depends upon the dynamics of 'power-shift'. Within the span of a few decades, a shift in the power is vividly and dramatically illustrated in the sphere of industrial relations. During the early phase of industrialization, if the managements indulged in exploitative control over labour, the growth of trade-union movements and the wave of welfare legislation had reversed the equations into a situation where the organized labour started holding the managements to ransom, in all sectors. This dramatic shift was illustrated by the statement of a trade-union leader (in response to a manager's observation that they are taking full care of the interests of the workers): "What have you given? We have fought for, and won". The process of economic liberalization is once again showing signs of restoration of the pre-existing imbalance in the form of disempowerment of the workers.

The constitutional amendment providing for constitutionally autonomous status to the Panchayati Raj institutions, with the centralized bureaucracy left untouched, and the recentralization of power in the political parties is yet another illustration of the dynamics of power shift. No wonder some of those who espouse the cause of the diverse range of human rights are described by some critics as the 'rights extremists'. It is in the same vein that the debate gets accentuated as to whether Naxalism is the 'cause' or 'consequence' of the distortions of democratic development.

A pluralist polity characterized by a commonality of goals and processes, over six decades, has been botched up with distorted and much abused concepts and labels such as 'secularism', reservations and minoritism to such an extent that the 'commonality' of nationality is reduced to fragmented identities and a fractured polity. Inspite of the communal politics, Indian polity retains its intrinsically 'secular' character.

The decisive reality is reduced to 'ruling' versus 'opposition' which are reinforced to such an extent that there are no limits to which political parties can go in creating social turbulence in order to run down the political party in power. A sick body-politic cannot develop immunities but will become an easy prey to the internal forces of anarchy and schism, much more than the external forces and factors of 'fundamentalism-extremism-terrorism' all in one. The targets of external or externally induced terrorists are the symbols of democracy i.e. legislatures, parliament, supreme/high court complexes, and institutions of science and technology and/or places of people's congregations apart from places of worship. It appears that we have not only not developed immunities, but we have evolved a political culture that has come to use 'conflict' as a means to secure and sustain political power. An enervated political leadership becomes vulnerable to the external forces of anarchy. When the popular psyche is ignited with hatred, the nation witnesses incidents such as in Delhi (1984), Mumbai (1992-93), Gujarat (2001) *et al.* The champions of 'secularism' by which they swear, in and out of context, do not recognize that casteism (and similar factors of schism) could become equally if not more, fatal to the democratic character of the country seeking to move together, towards a common set of goals and ideals of liberal democracy. The statistics of fatality and human distress caused by Delhi, Bombay and Gujarat, pale into insignificance when compared to the statistics and human degradation in a single state such as Bihar. It is strange that segmented champions of 'Minorities and Yadavs' (MY) spit fire in the name of a botched-up label of secularism. Buddhists who came out of Hinduism in protest against the caste system are today the neo-protagonists of a caste-based hierarchy. Dr. Ambedkar who gave up Hinduism in protest against caste-based oppression has been reduced a symbol of caste-based politics in India. Islam and Christianity are no exception to this phenomenon. Democracy in India has helped challenge the pre-existing hierarchies, but has generated, and aided the accentuation of social turbulence, hostility, conflict and violence. Can we call it a syndrome? India has yet to explore reliable and democratically tenable modes of change and harmony as the two sides of the same coin, viz., democratic development. In the emerging democracies, the states have failed in translating the democratic vision of promoting economic well being, delivering social justice and ensuring rule of law. Is it the exclusive function of policemen and police organizations to cleanse the un- and anti-democratic garbage?

The political leadership in India does not seem to recognize that they are chopping the branches of the same tree that they are perched on. The positive dynamic of Indian polity deserves reiteration that it reflects a robust democratic ethic. The need of the hour is leadership of institutions with a conviction and commitment to the vision of India, the constitutional focus of human development, and nation-building. Police, pitted against the multifarious anti-democratic forces, thus performing an increasingly critical role, have also to have an appreciation of India's constitutional democratic ethic.

In every society, and at all points of time, history has testified to the existence of 'conflict'. It is when such phenomenon gets aggregated and aggravated, it emerges as the Gross Social Conflict (GSC). In the Indian context the phenomenon of conflict – in terms of symptoms, manifestations and causal as well as contributory factors—can be analyzed as indicated in Illustration 5.

Democracy in Disarray

The Constitution has explicitly provided that it is the role of the judiciary to interpret the letter of the Constitution and to enforce the rule of law, apart from fulfilling an advisory role, when approached. In tune with the constitutional ethic, the judiciary has also responded to public outcry, in the form of Public Interest Litigation (PIL), against the political, legislative and executive institutions and thus saved the Republic from potential anarchy. The political and executive leadership instead of taking corrective measures have only started harping against judicial 'intervention',

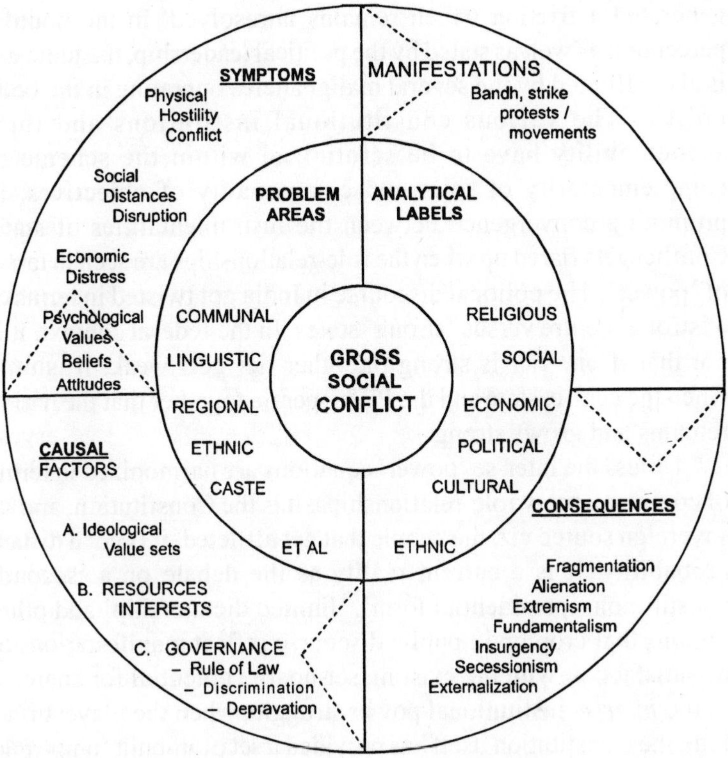

Illustration 5: Phenomena of Conflict

dubbing it on occasions, as judicial 'extremism' and 'adventurism'. There is a potentially dangerous deadlock. The assumed and occasionally asserted *inter-se* "supremacy" of the judiciary vis-à-vis the legislature also has contributed to serious proportions of institutional conflict in India. Most of the institutions set up under the provisions of the Constitution, such as the Tribes Advisory Councils (TACs) also got afflicted by the political malignancy. Police organizations seemingly are caught in the grip of 'ruling' political parties, which means shifting loyalties arising from electoral fortunes.

Partly arising from the distortions in the management of legislative institutions, and partly out of a misplaced perception and projection that the judiciary is 'supreme', the debate has generated a friction which remains unresolved. In the popular perception as well as stated by the political leadership, the judiciary is also afflicted by the several malignancies operating in the body politic. The various constitutional institutions and their accountability have to be scrutinized within the scheme of complementarity of roles and commonality of objectives, in promoting convergence between the instrumentalities of state. Conflict gets flared up when the role-relationships are seen in terms of 'power'. The political discourse in India got twisted in terms of a 'strong' centre versus 'strong' states. In the federal context, it is not that if one tier is strong the other tier gets weak. It is only when the centre, state and the PRIs operate together that the nation remains and grows strong.

Unless the inter-se 'power' equations are harmonized in terms of complementary role-relationships, it is the Constitution, and its sovereign source viz. the people that get afflicted; it is not a distant probability. It is a current reality as the debate on a 'second' constitution, 'presidential form', 'limited dictatorship' and other options that crop up in public discourse reflect manifestations of dissatisfaction with the existing set-up, the potential for anarchy. In the *inter se* institutional power struggle, when the players play foul, the Constitution itself has provided a set of in-built 'umpiring' roles such as the Speakers of legislatures, the Governors of states, the higher judiciary, especially the Supreme Court, as the final arbiter of the Constitution. Most important of all, and above all, it is the President who is the protector and defender of the Constitutional Republic. India has suffered the greatest conflict/, in the aggregate, as many of these umpires had failed, or worse, themselves faulted and played foul. Even the national legislature, by its commissions and omissions, had enervated the President of India.

The citizens of India have provided some correctives on many an occasion. But, the institutions which sought to protect their own privileges through an ill-defined set of norms, have expanded their contempt jurisdiction, choking the march of democracy. Commenting on the need for a resurrection of the rule of law, the eminent jurist V.R. Krishna Iyer lamented as to why the rule of law has gone berserk. And why has the legal system suddenly suffered a disaster syndrome vis-à-vis the countless masses? Today, the Indian Republic is in need of a legislative provision providing for 'contempt of the citizen.'

"The police entering the court halls (of the Madras High Court) attacking judges, lawyers, staff (with batons) and causing damage is a very serious matter", lamented one of the former Chief Justices of India. The prevailing nature of confrontation and conflict growing as between the instrumentalities of state is reflected in terms of centre vs. state, legislature vs. judiciary, generalists vs. specialists, IAS vs. IPS and most virulent of all viz., citizens vs. state. The urgent need to focus on the citizen in the Indian Republic also assumes significance not only due to the malfunctioning of the institutions, but the probability of the nation being washed away in the Tsunami of corruption leading to violent conflict and anarchy. At least two former Chief Ministers, while in office, had spurred the citizens, on two different occasions, to beat up the corrupt functionaries. The virus is so internalized and rapidly spreading all over, it is like the doctor catching the deadly virus.

The institutions of civil society have emerged the champions in promoting awareness among people, their participation, empowerment, equitable development, and in the aggregate as the bulwark of democracy and development. When they perform such a central role and also seek to provide correctives to the institutions of state, quite logically, in the face of an increasing crescendo of an conflict in society, some of the organizations of civil society are dubbed as 'rights' extremists and representatives of vested interests.

Conflict at any level – individual, inter-personal or inter-group — once it crosses the threshold of perception (taking the shape of fear, anxiety or tension, and prejudice) enters the phase of crystallized values, beliefs and enduring attitudes. Such attitudes create social distances in terms of "we" versus "they" leading to a heightened sense of insecurity, fright, verbal duel, imminence of violence, or get recorded as a 'memory', a landmark of an 'event of history', and thus become a part of group 'psyche'. Historical memories have emerged not merely in the form of a Mandir-Masjid conflict; they are kept alive and surface, as '*attitudinal*' dispositions, prejudices and behavioural triggers. It is this, 'embedded dispositions' that keeps alive and activates, like a volcano, labels such as "old city" in places like Ahmedabad, Hyderabad, New Delhi, *et al* and popular prejudices and hostile dispositions even during 'normal' times.

In the civilizational context, transcending the historical chapters, Indian society has its origins of *Sanatana Dharma*, as representing a way of life. During the times bygone, the territorial spread of Bharat was recorded as about 70,40,700 square kilometers. The emergence and spread of Islam as a religion was accompanied by territorial conquests, demolition of temples and debasement of *Sanatana Dharma*. Afghanistan, spread over 6,52,100 kilometers was carved out as a country from India. The spread or surge of the Muslim population continued far beyond the territory of Afghanistan, deeper and wider into the remaining 'territory' of 63,88,600 square kilometers.

It was the British who entered India as traders, turned rulers in order to suit their "control" and "administrative convenience" (historically labelled as "divide and rule") separated Sri Lanka in 1912, and Burma in 1948, with an area of 7,42,200 sq. km., further reducing India to 56,46,400 sq. km. Credit goes again to the British in meeting the challenge of Muslim minoritism by creating a sovereign territory of Pakistan on the Western and Eastern flaps of Bharat. With the creation of Pakistan, spread over 4,32,200 sq. km. there was further shrinking of Bharat's territory.[12]

Mobility of population, for education and in search of opportunities for livelihood, across political, national and cultural boundaries has been a constant in human history and civilization. It is in this context that Neil Armstrong, the first human to set foot on the planet moon, had stated that his landing represented a giant step for humanity. Diverse patterns of migration were promoted by governments (indentured labour and incentives for skilled resources) regulated or prohibited. As a part of the process of acquisition of lands to set up industrial, infrastructural and other 'development' projects, people have been displaced, their livelihoods and communitarian lifestyles disrupted; people were reduced to the state of refugees of development. There is an enormous growth of social strife. Governments have not yet recognized the need to mainstream the people. In such a situation of state-generated social strife, people are either 'organizing' themselves and triggering resistance and destruction or rushing towards the judiciary for justice.

Judicial institutions are thus drawn into this vortex of charge in diverse mutations, such as public interest litigation, judicial intervention, activism and extremism leading to confrontation. The judicial system itself is being dragged into this vortex as witnessed in the High Courts of Chennai and Andhra Pradesh. Such malfunctioning of the instrumentalities of state affects not only the vehicle, but the constitutional journey itself.

Influx of Bangladeshis and Jihadi activists into Assam, gradually spreading almost to all the states, admittedly due to a failure in containing this influx, at the same time extending liberally voting rights as a part of vote-bank politics, even after the Supreme Court's intervention, has been changing the demography of not only the region but of the country as a whole. Induced and aggressive religious conversions of Hindus to not only Islam but also the Christian faith and many more factors and processes have rapidly deteriorated the secular (inter-religious) equations, leading to conflicts and flares of violence. It is not just induced and organized conversions on a massive scale, but the methods and modes of such conversion – right within the precincts of Hindu temples, dumping money from Islamic and Christian organizations into India, India being seen as the largest mass with no resistance, Indianized projection of the Bible, sari-clad Virgin Mary and many more factors have grossly increased the level and intensity of communal identities, hostile attitudes as well as conflict, undermining the democratic fabric of India.

In the absence of precise operationalization the concept, secularism, has turned into a chameleon. Religion, secularism, and communalism have become the most misused and abused expressions – leading to an aggregation of pseudo secularism. That the entire spectrum of political parties has not so far cared for, much less responded to the opinion of the Supreme Court that the concept has to be operationalized so as to evolve a uniform meaning suggests that the existing confusion provides pliable interpretations and practices that suit the partisan political convenience, with potential turbulence in the polity.

Ayodhya presents a two-in-one case of demolition of a temple as well as a Masjid. The public debate continues to an ever-increasing pitch, encompassing inter-faith relations, high levels of 'anxiety neurosis' and accentuated conflict among all communities leading to aggressive demands for state intervention against religious conversions, and private protection from fundamentalist groups. Emergence of Hindu suicide squads occupies the secular space of Indian democracy.

The states are responsible and accountable for the maintenance of law and order. Diverse ground conditions on this count leads to the threat of central intervention, with dramatic and traumatic implications for the federal equations of the polity. Police as the professional organization entrusted with the task of law and order does not appear to be playing any role in the proclamation of President's Rule under Article 356 of the Constitution. Curiously, such proclamations, ostensibly based on failure of law and order, have not reflected on the role, status and efficacy of police performance.

Have the police organizations in India come to appreciate the phenomena of democracy, which encompasses the dynamic process of social transformation and participative governance? What had been the role of police (as a 'peace force') envisioned in the constitutional democracy in India? Have the police 'attuned', themselves to such a 'role-shift', from the colonial rule to the democratic process? Does policing in a democracy call for the transformation of its police?

Even after the advent of constitutional democracy, police continued with the tradition of respecting the 'autonomous' character of educational institutions, like a university. But today, we have police stations or outposts in most of the universities. Police are compelled to enter the universities to tackle turbulence on the campuses, created by the students as well as the teachers, often with support from the mainline political parties. Police have either entered or were summoned into the premises of High Courts, and the legislatures, which are the sanctified institutions of democracy. With the emergence of private armies and –'arms-bazars', our nascent democracy has acquired facets of barbarian civilization. No doubt we in India are training our people to face nuclear, biological and chemical calamities and disasters, but, have we thought of the need to prepare the police to handle situations of political turmoil, fist fights and the use of IEDs within the environs of legislatures? Have the police organizations and police think tanks attempted and projected futuristic scenarios of peace, violence and security? Does policing in a democracy call for, as a prerequisite, democratizing the police forces as a part of a comprehensive political economic, social and legal process that is timely and appropriate? In the face of the increasing crescendo of social turbulence and conflicts leading to violence, have our police forces explored peace initiatives so as to contribute to the protection of our democratic fabric? Contemporary democratic eruption everywhere in the world provides insights into the potential conditions. Perhaps, police in India have to go beyond ideas such as minority police, tribal battalions, and women police stations. The most important and critical role of the police (leadership) is to examine how policing has to be changed, and to educate the people. Police leadership, as professionals, owe it to themselves to play a critical role in shaping the way policing is done in India.

During the first six decades (which can be described as the take off decades of democracy in India) the demos may have faltered, but woke up to the distortions caused by the malignant factors of the political system. These distortions in the democratic process have however awakened the people to generate pressure on the political system towards course corrections. Political leadership have started recognizing that the time for change has come. The political statement that "we have to change the way policing is done" in our democracy is, in part, an acknowledgement of the canvas and context of the change process. Unlike a pedal boat, an ocean liner needs careful manoeuvreing; larger space and longer time to turn around. That is the democratic challenge facing the prime movers and the police professionals in India. They have to prepare an action plan and a time frame, to bring about that change. Time is not on their side.

2

Security Scenario: 'Red' Alert – A Constant

Conceptual: Doctrinal : Empirical Facets of Security

The phenomenon of security is fascinatingly complex, for academicians as well as 'specialists', who are also referred to as experts. For the policy makers and the administrators, the phenomena of security offers itself as a challenge, akin to making an omelette without breaking the egg. The phenomenon of 'security' can be considered operating at the level of every individual human being, expanding in concentric circles, at diversely (aggregated) levels, such as a family, community, nation, continent or global society.

The twentieth century has witnessed the emergence of democracy on a global scale, hailed as though it represents the 'end of history', as an ideology. Democracy as an ideal solution to the problems of human organization and as an appropriate process that would help build a society as a nation on a sustainable basis has also signalled the movement towards globalization of economies. This process of globalization has contributed to a 'confluence' as well as a 'clash' of cultures. Even as the 'national' boundaries seem to be melting as a result of globalization and liberalization, conflicts between communities within, as well as across the nations, are growing complex.

At the threshold of the 21st century, human civilization is witnessing a crescendo of social strife. If we piece together all the perceptions (coloured by the milieu of individual and group values, beliefs, interests, identities and historical experiences), like in the story of seven blind persons trying to describe an elephant, we see all colours and diverse perceptions merging to reflect the security scenario. In such a situation, identification of individual shades does not seem logical or feasible. Devoid of legalese and jargon, the ever expanding dimensions of security can be 'operationalized' in terms of (a) conflicts of values, (b) clash of interests, and (c) crises of identities, spread in concentric circles, within or across national boundaries, activating an interaction of political, economic, socio-cultural and ethnic factors. Such an interaction and its spread-effect are often accentuated by inadequacies in the functioning of institutions and processes of governance on one hand and hostile actions of 'external' forces on the other. This phenomenon gestates as tensions in the society, manifest in diverse forms such as extremism, terrorism and fundamentalism, and gets triggered to explode into violence, affecting internal equilibrium of communities as much as the stability of institutions of state and society.

We are entering into an era where the entire concept of security will change, and change dramatically: (i) security of people, not just security of territory; (ii) security of ethnic groups, not just security of their nations; (iii) security through development not merely through arms; (iv) security of all people everywhere in their homes, in their jobs, in their streets, in their communities (festivals, cultural events), in their environments.[13] Prachanda, the revolutionary leader of 'Maoists' movement in Nepal, who fought the established socio-political order for decades and won 'democratic' 'liberation' for the people, lamented after assuming office as Prime Minister of the nascent democracy, that it is easy to wage an insurgency 'war' and change the political order but that, when it comes to the fruits of war, the substance of economic growth and social development, the newly emerging democracies have no option but to follow the path and modes of development as dictated by the western dominated global institutions like the World Bank. Social turbulence continues but assumes a different manifestation and complex form.

The political, economic and cultural 'dominance' of the west, perceived or real, has combined into a single but strong strand of resentment and anger especially among the Islamic populations around the world. This hostility against the west is also accentuated due to a perception of the relative failure of their own societies; the west came handy to blame for their own shortcomings. The second wave of the Islamic *Jihadi* world appears to have found legitimacy beyond expectations in the wake of aggressive actions of the west against the oil-rich Arabs, and the Islamic world as the terrorist spring board. The cultural dimension of conflict has transformed and expanded into inter-state as well as into state-versus-civil-society conflict.

With its origins in an innocuous place, Naxalism, spread its flares to several states, such as Andhra Pradesh, Madhya Pradesh, Bihar, West Bengal, Chhattisgarh, Jharkhand and Orissa within India, and found its confluence with Maoism in Nepal. Like the unpredictable path and intensity of a cyclonic storm, conflicts develop their own paths and hit the coast with varying intensity; like cyclones violent movements do not recognize state boundaries; conflicts defy geographical frontiers.

As the world has come to learn from 9/11, aggression need not originate from trained military personnel but men and women with enough fanatical devotion. The battlefields of the 21st century range from scorching deserts to the virtual landscape of cyber space. Nuclear, Chemical, Biological and Radiological Weapons are added to traditional tactical weapons. 'Non-lethal Weapons' such as rubber bullets, sten guns, and sticky foam *et al* add to the hostile security environment even while reducing the number of casualties that normally result from 'military' and 'militant' combat.[14] The process of concentric expansion assuming the pattern of the 'big bang' where the diverse elements are inter-connected and interact, would never 'settle-down' to a frozen pattern.

The nature of conflict as a manifestation of insecurity, has been changing along with the diverse modes of conflict. During the phase of colonialism, competition in trade, acquisition of territory and protecting the interests of the empire prompted the build-up of the police force. But with the 'national' communities waking up, liberation movements and political 'freedom' spreading across the globe, the dominant powers became conscious of the costs (political, economic as well military) of holding on to territories. Multi-National Corporations (MNCs) that perceived populous countries as growing markets have come to replace the armies. Capitalism justified profits, global competition, and market domination. In the emerging global context, the 20th century Brettonwood institutions of global governance (WTO, IMF, WB, UNSC) et al, provided the normative base and institutional mechanisms to protect the interests of the developed, dominant powers at the expense of the developing nations. When migration from the poorer regions became necessary to man the process and pace of growth of the developed nations, it generated culture conflict/s, the concept of Business Process Outsourcing (BPO) was innovated so as to reduce culture-conflict and yet protect the economic interests (TRIPS, IPR) as well as the cultural exclusivity of the capitalistic, western, developed national communities. The cultural divide got aggravated by an interconnected cause and effect series of crusades and *Jihads*, apart from factors such as forced and induced religious conversions leading to the clash of civilizational dimensions. The contemporary conflict in human society in the form of extremism, terrorism, fundamentalism, and others represents the manifestations and mutations of conflict and violence rooted in and emerging from the diverse facets of 'security'.

Unquestioning ethnocentric faith in the moral stances and cultural superiority of communities, conditioned by different climes and times, have critically contributed to cultural retreats and myriad forms of conflicts. Talibanization of the Islamic communities reinforced with the revival of public flogging, discriminatory practices against women, such as denial of modern education, destruction of sites, such as Bamiyan Buddhist sculptures represent violent extremism.

Within India, the demolition, nay destruction of places (temples) of religious sanctity such as the Lord Ram Temple in Ayodhya, Lord Krishna Temple in Mathura, and that of Lord Siva in Varanasi as a part of Islamic invasion, and construction of structures, Islamic structures, with the same material on the same sites has generated Hindu-Muslim hostilities and remained embedded in the Hindu psyche leading to retaliatory demolition of the Babri Masjid and demands for the reconstruction of the 'Ram Mandir. Such long standing reciprocal hostile attitudes, generate dispositions of religious extremism and fundamentalism. Depicting the images of religious symbols (images of revered gods and goddesses) of Hindus on the lingerie, socks and chappals add fuel to the fire of historical memories and plague the pluralist character of Indian democracy. Ram *Sena's* violent attacks on a group of girls enjoying their 'freedom' and free time in a pub emerges as yet another manifestation of 'intolerance' of one cultural group against what they consider an alien cultural value, as an assault on Indian culture. In such situations of culture conflict, culture policing slips into the hands of private-citizen groups pitted against fellow citizens.

Indifference, benign negligence and callousness on the part of the political leadership and institutions of governance to act in good time leads to situations where the Union Home Minister had categorically stalled (4 May 2012) on the floor of the Rajya Sabha that "any citizen belonging to the north-eastern states is free to travel and reside in any part of the country", and went on as if to clarify or remind the State Governments that they are "obliged to ensure their safety and security". He could have such a normative guideline to all the states of India in the context of the regional, linguistic and ethnic maze of multi-dimensional conflicts in India today.

That even international terror is an offshoot of domestic innocuous looking outfits such as the students Islamic Movement of India (SIMI) reveals the complexity of the security scenario, where social conflict can be triggered as a nation-wide menace.

India today represents a sick body, infested with multiple diseases, fractures and loss of immunities, a billion rich citizenship, pitted against itself. It may not have become a failed state, but a soft state has become a turbulent state. With a political culture that can be encapsulated in one word as 'Biharization', citizens are alienated from the state and have turned hostile. With ill-defined role-clarity as between the Union and the States, Indian society is yearning to become dynamic by redefining and redesigning the role of extant static organizations.

Though security, conflict and violence constitute a global phenomena, the manifestations can be 'enumerated' in the context of the Indian setting. The 'problem' areas, the diverse facets, the territorial spread of these problems, and their external linkages are indicated in Illustration 6.

Sl. No.	*Problems*	*Facets*	*Territory : External linkages*
1	2	3	4
1	Partition Communalization Social Fragmentation	Historical memories Illiteracy Social prejudices	Globalization Democratization Liberalization
2	Caste Conflict Ethnic Conflict Culture Policing	International / Alliances	AP BH UP TN MP
3	Distortions of Development Liberalization	Alienation Farmers' suicides Reservation Market wars Corruption	Backward areas Backward people
4	Regionalism Separatism / Autonomy	Political schism Socio-economic ills Culture conflict Small states	MS AP WB NE BH MP UP
5	Extremism Terrorism Fundamentalism	Insurgency Secessionism Tribal Home Land	PB JK NE TN DL Support from neighbours World Terrorists Meet LTTE ISI
6	Secular Discourse Communal Conflict	Forced conversions	UP BH AP RJ TN MS GJ MP OR
7	Corruption Counterfeit Arms bazars	Money laundering Black money Kick-backs	External-Internal Continuum

Illustration 6: Security Scenario – Age of Uncertainty: Action-Related Cycles

The ever-changing ground conditions and the dynamic factors at play contributing to the concept and modus of conflict defy any static classification and categorization of 'security'. It is the dynamic threat factors that are leading the national strategies and security forces. The conversion process of primary, secondary and tertiary factors of conflict, is a function of the nature and degree of politicization as an intervening variable, and demonstrates that complex phenomena cannot be explained in terms of a single causal factor. It is seen that situations ripen over a period of time, and with the accretion, and aggregation of intervening factors, conflict builds up and explodes into violent tremors or quakes, almost in a 'predictable' manner and pattern. What is predictable can be measured on a scale of conflict, even under dynamic conditions. The behaviour of people, at individual as well as group levels, however, cannot be explained in terms of any single factor causation, in isolation.

Kashmir represents a three-in-one freedom movement, fundamental rights and terrorist-supported armed conflict. Where there is a conflict, there are alliances such as in J & K where (self-appointed) leaders of Naxalism or civil rights movements see tactical advantages that can be exploited. Political party leaders look at problems of conflict in society as opportunities to be 'exploited'; and they do exploit, mostly young people.

A Bench of the Supreme Court comprising Justice B. Sudarshan Reddy and S.S. Nijjar, hearing (8 Mar 2011) a petition filed by one-time Union Law Minister Ram Jethmalani on the Union governments alleged inaction to retrieve black money stashed away abroad, asked the Solicitor General (Gopal Subrahmanian) to explain the Government's stand at the next hearing (on March 18). Justice Reddy told the Solicitor General that there were reports about a fake passport case against the accused (Hasan Ali Khan), and asked him (SG) to "examine whether the CBI can undertake this probe." There are (media) reports suggesting that the accused (Hasan Ali Khan) is linked to international arms dealer (Adnan Khassogi). Justice Sudarshan Reddy continued that "there is possibly a national security angle. This matter be probed under provisions other than of the Prevention of Money Laundering Act, the Passport Act and the Foreign Exchange Management Act. Can you invoke anti-terror law, perhaps under the state law? We feel those are far more serious than Income Tax Violation."[15]

The conceptual elements, dimensions and the frontiers of 'security' are dynamic, presenting a situation of constant flux. How does one take stock of those frontiers and elements in a holistic manner? These elements have been identified variously, in terms of (a) levels of causal factors, such as primary, secondary and tertiary; (b) ivory-tower analytical labels such as the political, the economic, the social, the cultural, the administrative, (c) in the jurisprudential categorization emerging from penal code and criminal procedures, and as reflected by, (d) the chronological, historical evolutionary phases. All these typologies would be valid and relevant in their own place. The complex reality of security defies all the exclusivist explanations as the complex reality is characterized by interacting sets of factors. The elements of the security scenario are akin to cluster-bombs, triggering a chain reaction of social turbulence, disruption and destruction, leading to a series of sustained after-effects. These mutually interacting and constantly changing 'triggers' can be labeled in terms of (a) values forming a part of acculturation (b) perceptions and prejudices emerging from experiences leading to ideological dispositions of individuals or groups, and diverse range of conflicting 'issues', (c) ever-changing socio-economic factors and interests, and (d) innovations in science and technology, as they are manipulated or abused by humans.

If Louai Al-sakka the alleged Al-Qaeda operative, on trial for orchestrating the 2003 Istanbul bombings, (after refusing to stand to address the judge in a Turkish court room) stated that "I performed jihad and killed Americans! Why should I stand up in front of you?" The dynamic characteristic of conflict in society, and its passive and active states, like a volcano can be graphically described as the 'Spin of Conflict' as in Illustration 7. Each eruption of conflict on any issue in any society creates flares in the immediate vicinity of time and space; these flares in course of time generate the spin effect, and leave a residue as accretion to the core of conflict in the society. These flares can be tracked,

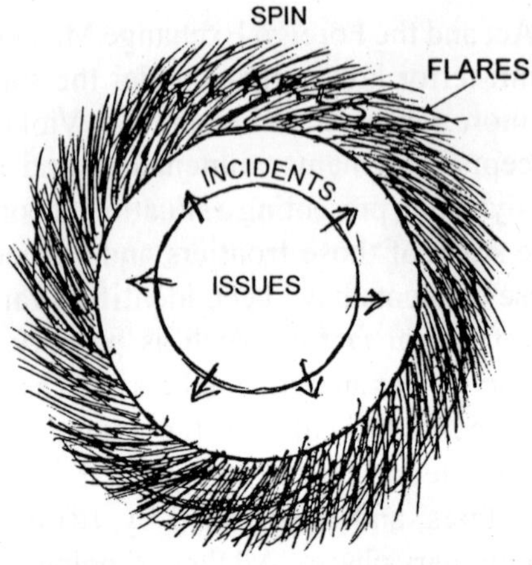

Illustration 7: Spin of Conflict

measured with their intensity over time and space almost like in a seismic zone. The most proximate examples of such flares in the Indian context are 1984 (Delhi), 1992 (Babri), 2002 (Gujarat), and many more.

Seismic disasters cannot be prevented but mitigation measures can be formulated with a target of zero loss of life. Conflict flares and zones can be predicted and thus it is possible, even if difficult, but not impossible to aim at zero loss of life. Reflecting on the human history of the 20th century the Harvard Research Centre on creative alternatives as a part of studies of the eminent writer Pitirim Sorokin observed: "During this period, a legion of "liberators", "leaders" and groups moved predominantly by hate, lust for domination and by individual/collective egotism, have attempted either to maintain the existing "decent order" or to build a nobler and better millennium in the human universe. They attempted to do this mainly by the method of unlimited violence and mass extermination of all their enemies and opponents through the world wars and "small wars", bloody revolutions and counter revolutions, brutal revolutions and merciless suppressions. In the name of the "Fatherland" and the "International" "Capitalism" and "Communism", "Autocracy" and "Democracy", "Republic" and "Monarchy", "Atheism" and "Religion", "Freedom" and

"Sovereignty", more than sixty millions of human beings, including innocent children, women and old people have been slaughtered, many other millions have been maimed and have prematurely died, thousands of cities and villages have been turned into "abomination of desolation", numberless unspeakable bestialities have been perpetrated, and an immeasurable amount of suffering has been inflicted upon mankind".[16]

The Indian constitution has promised a massive range and scale of human rights. Sixty years of democratic governance has proved too short to translate and transform promise into a reality for successive governments had indulged in knee-jerk initiatives in this direction. Consequently what we witness today is reduced to an unending saga of human rights and growing (a) gap between promise and performance, and (b) growing conflict around human rights.

Internal-External Continuum

Democracy that has surged during the 20th century swept most of the Asian and African continents and the Soviet Union as the 'ultimate', 'ideal' model of social organization. By itself, it may represent an evolutionary model, but the surge of democracy can uproot and wash away anything and everything that comes in and obstructs its path and pace. Thus, democratic transitions, especially those like in India which are multi-layered and seeking to build upon secular cultures, can be traumatic and destructive too, adding to the challenge of change. Once the democratic form is attained, the actual process of transformation can be a painful and prolonged phase, the state of 'bleeding democracy'. It is in the hope of containing this bleeding, through the process of social transformation and nation building, that the 20th and 21st century democratizing countries, have taken the path of liberalization aspiring to register faster and higher levels of economic 'growth', as an aid to democratic social transformation. But, the processes of globalization, liberalization and privatization have intensified the transitional trauma and the bleeding state of democratic transition.

This rapid and rabid liberalization moved faster than Indian democracy and society could absorb and integrate, what with the institutions of mal-governance infested by the political malignancies that have exposed India's bleeding democracy to the onslaught of MNCs. The MNCs have defied and defiled Indian political, economic, social and cultural facets of the democratic process, and without an adequate and efficient regulatory mechanism in place, have trespassed even the legal system, both civil and criminal, in a manner contemptuous of Indian democracy. Economic and corporate policies and practices, especially in regard to human resources development and management, have added to the trauma of transition. Human distress took the place of human development, the core of democratization under the Constitution of India. A nascent democracy seeking to grow into a great nation was reduced to a bulging market. The whole spectrum of industrialization has become an issue of law and order, turning India into a malignant and violent democracy.

When crime, politics, and business, have established an entrenched alliance democratic development is high-jacked, not only in India, but in almost all democracies as well as other forms of political organizations – it is the consequent distortions and shortcomings that had warranted the Prime Ministers and Presidents of the comity of nations to meet at Copenhagen under the auspices of the United Nations to address the problems of the distortions of the democratic process – and unanimously agreed to set up, at their own respective national levels, Commissions of Social Development so as to fuse growth with development, and thus prevent and contain turbulence and violence.

There is a 'universality' of threat to the challenge of democratic transformation, arising from an alliance between the 'internal' and 'external' factors of security as a continuum. There are no 'internal' groups, organized (or not so organized) adopting the agenda of 'alternative' modes of development, without any international alliances, interactions and/or transactions – ideological, operational and tactical. In fact, there seems to be better coordination and cooperation between these 'organizations', in regard to training, arms supplies and tactical support. With 13,960 police stations spread over 626 districts in the 26 states and 5 union territories, intelligence reports point out that left wing extremism has spread over 20 states. While some commentators prefer to refer to LWE as a spillover of distortions of development, some others wonder whether peace with Maoists can ever be achieved.

Democracies are pitted against undemocratic and anti-democratic forces within; democracies have to observe the democratic ethic and rules of the game, but the anti-democratic forces by their very nature, do not have to follow the rules of the game, they make their own rules, and impose some of their own, on the democracies. It is an uneven battle.

Conflict and violence that had afflicted public order, peace, democratic fabric of the country and the nation building process have been brought into the political cauldron. Issues such as communalism, caste, linguistic aspirations, ethnic unrest, class clashes, spiced by extremism, secessionism, and terrorism, are challenging the modes and methods of democratic governance. A democratic surge of human rights and political entitlements, mal-governance, and commissions and omissions of police have all added to the nature, complexity and magnitude of law and order, and national security.

Public administration which has not yet shed off its colonial character, has been assigned, overnight, the role as 'managers of change', a task they were not prepared for, and perhaps being unwilling for such transformation, retain their Weberian character, and impede democratic power shift.

The fundamental right of all citizens to follow their religion, culture and to express their views have been mixed up with a 'right' to inducing people forcibly for a consideration, in cash or kind, to convert to another religion. It is a socio-politically modified gene, exclusive to India. When the state fails to contain this campaign, social tempers and tensions rise. Religion gets reduced to 'communalism'. If there is a naked motivation in the minds of the 'campaigners' to swell the 'partisan' and 'prejudiced' ratios of people, fear and hatred coalesce to engender violence and conflict. It reaches the peak breakdown point, when campaigns for conversion take the form not only of commending one religion but also condemning another religion. It spurs as a license to disrupt public order and to destroy rule of law. A group of goons can burn and destroy public property. The 'ruling' party instead of ensuring that law takes its own course, haplessly explains such lawlessness as an "emotional response and hence condonable by the state". Such distortions and inactions lead to negative images and dispositions towards police. Legislators, belonging to the minority, open fire on public servants on duty, and get away unchecked; but decisively to leave a negative perception of law and order management. Not allowing law to take its course leads to mal-governance, Such compromises on the part of the state with law enforcement, prompt different social groups to take to violence in a recurrent manner. Violence yields political dividends.

The internal spectrum of security, especially in multi-cultural, democracies like India gets accentuated by many an "external" factor expanding the internal spectrum into an external continuum. International and global organizations create indigenous terrorist organizations like Students Islamic Movement of India (SIMI), feed and 'operate' (the more appropriate expression could be 'manipulate') them as the extended units of terrorism. SIMI proved a perfect recruitment agency for the Indian Mujahideen that claimed responsibility for as many as nine terrorist actions spread over as many states during a short span of time from 2007 to 2010. The Vatican's concerns about Catholics in Pakistan, the rise of Muslim brotherhood as a global phenomenon, foreign vessels in the Bay of Bengal, absconding Bangla nationals taking shelter in places like Hyderabad (AP), fears of radical takeover of nuclear weapons in Pakistan, the US Congressional hearings on radicalization and "demonizing" Muslims, and many more 'developments' melt the illusions of differentiation between the external and the internal dimensions of security, and transform them into a single spectrum of national security.

As violence spreads, grows and intensifies, the police are restrained. When violence sustains itself, to a point where it becomes too hot for political bosses, the police are asked to declare Section 144, issue a red-alert, or worse 'shoot at sight'. Public unrest and violence provokes police 'excesses' (such as use of excessive force, converting itself as a 'lathi-force'), indiscriminate beating of the people to pulp, mass-scale arrests, indiscriminate firing, abuse of women in prisons *et al.* Indian democracy is converted into a 'breeder-reactor' of conflict and violence; worse, prejudices are frozen, breeding hostile attitudes. When there is such massive, sustained violence in some of the 'developed' democracies, such violence is explained away. But in the case of democracy in India, different brand names and labels are affixed to situations of conflict.

Distorted images of democracy lead to negative perceptions beyond the boundaries. UNDP (HDI Report 2004) has observed: "Rise of the Hindu groups which seek to impose a singular religion in the country posed a threat to social harmony" and similar other comments, such as "Hindu extremists have fomented anti-Muslim violence in Gujarat even as Muslim extremists have targeted Hindus" as also ad hoc and random reflections such as: "India's challenge was in reinvigorating (India's) commitment to practices of pluralism, institutional accommodation and conflict resolution through democratic means". Such random concerns do not square up with the Directive Principle in regard to a uniform civil code and religion-based reservations. Efforts such as the Bush administration's observation that India has returned 'to a position that is more secular' after the exit of the BJP-led government, and its 2004 Report on Global Religious Freedom while expanding the debate to a global scale, leads to branding of the half-baked concept of secularism. When the drag factors of democracy are allowed to slide to untenable levels, where the external commentators describe India as a 'functional anarchy', and as a 'soft-state', it gets reduced to a sick-state, a bleeding democracy; like a wounded body it invites infections. India had to defend itself on the Human Rights record during the Universal Periodic Review (UPR) convened by the Human Rights Council (HRC) in Geneva (May, 2012). During the review, the civil society organizations expressed their dissatisfaction of India's presentation, led by its Attorney General.

The National Security Strategy clearly states: "Terrorists are organized to penetrate open societies and to turn the power of modern technologies against us. To defeat this threat we must make use of every tool in our arsenal – military power, better homeland defences, law enforcement, intelligence and vigorous efforts to cut off terrorists' financing. The war against terrorists of global reach is a global enterprise of uncertain duration".[17] India is yet to learn from its own experience and put into practice without any dangerous hesitation, a conscious, consensual strategy in place. The debate, the nagging-dragging debate over the National Counter Terrorism Centre testifies the Indian reality.

The external forces had declared that they will "stop the heart of India from beating". Security forces, gallant, disciplined and dedicated as they are, can contain terrorism, even with shortage of equipment. But, where terrorism is spread through 'in-house' forces and local networks, that operate with impunity, such 'extremism' generates limits to tolerance, and hostility gets accentuated not only against such external terrorist organizations but also 'Hindu Taliban', 'non-state actors', 'Bajrang Bali', 'external funding' of local networks, 'training bases', 'safe-havens and shelters' and unholy alliances between extremists and terrorists across boundaries emerge as the logical consequence, all leading to an accentuation of unpredictable patterns, modes and magnitude of conflict destructive of 'democracy', a whole nation.

It is a fallacy to delineate 'internal' and 'external' security as if these are two different sets. National security is a single phenomenon, a continuum. The sources can be categorized into two sets viz., those germinated, nurtured and located outside the national boundaries, and those inside the boundaries. Even this classification / categorization may prove fallacious. Land surface may be demarcated and identified as acres of gardens, but the roots of the trees would grow sub-terraneously, defying external demarcations. ISI, LTTE, and LeT have strong sub-terraneous roots; they would not terrorist organizations if they don't have such roots.

Global terrorists all over have not been found wanting in the exploitation of S&T advances in spheres such as the nuclear, chemical, biological and radiological warfare in achieving a punch in cross border terrorism. Indeed the national boundaries have started melting to the advantage of terrorist organizations. Embedded chips and electronic terrorism are effectively being used by the terrorists; in fact the terrorists are innovating and applying frontier technologies in the course of home-grown as well as global terror. One of the masterminds of the 9/11 attacks in the USA (Khalid Sheikh Mohammed) alleged to have close links with Saifullah Paracha, had allegedly plotted to smuggle chemical, biological and radioactive materials into the US for attacks. "According to classified US diplomatic cables released by Wikileaks, Pakistan President Asif Ali Zardari told US Vice President Joe Biden of his fear that the Pakistani military might "take me out". And the United Arab Emirates Foreign Minister told US Special Envoy Richard C. Holbrooke in early 2015 that Zardari had asked "that his family be allowed to live in the UAE in the event of his death". In such a deviant setting, the fear that the *jihadis* within the military could gain control of Pakistan's arsenal of nuclear and biological weapons are real".[18] There is mounting evidence, surfacing with an ever-increasing frequency, that recruiters for Islamist terror groups have targeted the information technology sphere giving a bit of boost and a technological edge to the jihadi movement as well as other extremist groups.

Democracy in India provides a 'soft state' syndrome which is being exploited to the hilt by the global terrorist groups. In the wake of increasing terrorist activities and episodes, Home Ministers as well as Directors General of Police have given a clean chit to themselves that their respective states are not safe havens to terrorist operations, only to follow up such statements with a declaration of their intent to uproot 'solvent' terrorism with all the might of the state. The Indian state, or states to be precise, had always ended up declaring a red alert and a comprehensive plan to address the phenomena of terrorism, demanded and obtained hundreds of crores of rupees for the 'modernization' of the police (though not spent all the funds so allocated). The declaration of (Red) Alert itself has become a frequent affair; so frequent that it has amounted to a false cry, when it is seriously warranted, so it may not serve the intended purpose, though it never has been lifted formally. Chris Smith of the London-based Center for Defence Studies observes:

"US diplomat Robert Oakley felt the US had failed in Vietnam because of excessive interference and micro-management. So in the case of Pakistan and Afghanistan he instituted the exact reverse: no accountability, macro-management and non-interference.... The logic of this *laissez-faire* policy was completely unsuited to the culture and history of the region, notorious for corruption, gun-culture and smuggling."

"Militants also enjoy secure bolt-holes and training camps across the line-of-control into Azad Kashmir. The training camps are said to be run by the ISI, staffed by both Taliban and Afghan training officers."

"There is evidence that extremists as well as mercenaries from other countries, such as Sudan and Afghanistan, are filtering across the border. In the wake of the Afghan war there are a large number of Muslims in the region intent on joining the nearest *Jihad* and Kashmir is an appropriate location."

"In Pakistan, the ISI have largely pursued their own national and foreign policies, which have included providing weapons and training for Kashmiri and Punjabi militant groups since the early '80s. The ISI still appear to have access to sufficient firepower to destabilize both Pakistan and India."[19]

Bus loads of Pakistanis arriving in the Chakota area in Pakistan occupied Kashmir attempting to cross and infiltrate. Pakistan was interested in making political capital out of the prevailing situation in the Kashmir valley, by rousing the people and bringing them on the streets; spreading rumours about the holy relic at Hazratbal, to inflame passions by throwing torn pages of the Holy Quran near bunkers manned by security forces.

Reflecting on the cyclical phenomenon of causes and consequences, the Governor of J & K observed that the residents of the Valley "were apprehensive . . . . the *Ekta Yatra* could lead to more efforts to do away with (constitutional) safeguards available to the Kashmiris. The Judicial process in the valley had broken down and no lawyer was prepared to take up cases on behalf of the Government. Witnesses were afraid to appear in cases where militants had committed crimes. The local police are afraid of taking action against the militants. The security forces are fighting a proxy war . . . the process of law proceeds at a slow pace. We don't find even judges to try cases in which militants are involved".[20] Precisely these consequences constituted the goals of militant action from across the border.

Indian coastal security has been grossly breached in Mumbai during Nov 2008. It has opened up possible attacks from airborne platforms similar to the 9/11 attacks in the US. Though it is not an attack by the armed forces of an enemy country, such an attack amounts to nothing less than a war. It is admitted openly that (a) Simi and Indian Mujahideen and other terrorist groups are funded by external sources like LeT – in many a form and channel, including charity; (b) these terrorist groups swear that "the dust will never settle down" and that (c) Al-Qaeda instructors have trained the Mumbai (Nov 2008) attackers; (d) that some of the Gulf countries provide safe havens for the Islamic terrorists (including those from India) to park, plan and operate from their territories; (e) these terrorists have extensive links to organized crime within the Indian territory; (f) the Lashkari-trained Indian terrorists operate from their home i.e. Indian territory, with impunity.

A new breed of Muslim warrior has arrived on this planet. He operates all over the globe, fired by religious zeal. Such a brand of Islamic extremist turned terrorist has become a 'model' for diverse organizational mutations. An alliance of the unholy, a network of local alliances gelling into a global alliance has emerged towards the close of the 20th century, which doesn't recognize national or cultural boundaries. The local outfits and alliances may have their own 'agenda' but the alliance *'Dharma'* is based on their method viz., 'extremism' and terrorism.

During August 1996, some of world's most dangerous terrorists and their apologists had gathered in London, UK, for a conference aimed at forming a platform to get rid of "anti-Islamic States".[21] *The Times* report said: "Representatives from groups convicted of planning the bombing of the World Trade Centre in New York, Beirut based Hezbollah, Hamas, Algerian Muslim Brotherhood and shadowy Mujhaddin groups of Afghanistan have sent video messages calling for global holy war." A 'rally of revival' conference was planned to be staged in east London with more than 14,000 Muslim activists expected to attend, the newspaper said. The event was organized by Omar Bakri, former leader of the Hizb-ul-Tahrir whose organization had been banned from a large number of campuses across Britain for his reported call for assassination of the then British Prime Minister, John Major and called for struggle against the Jewish and the Hindu students. *The Times* quoted intelligence and police officials expressing concern over such rallies, which would bring ultra fundamentalist groups together under the banner of 'Khalifate', a single Muslim state. The paper said, prominent figures who would speak at the conference (through video recording) included the shadowy Saudi fundamentalist group financier, Sheikh Osman Bin Laden, who was killed by the American forces, in Abbotabad on the outskirts of Islamabad, capital of Pakistan during 2011.

On the basis of an indepth analysis of the phenomenon of terror, Ranjan Roy observes "The spine chilling Beslam massacre in Russia is over: Terrorism has once again reared its hydra heads. But contrary to the blinkered vision of the US, terrorism is not always spawned by Muslims; take the IRA, the LTTE or the Aum Shinrikhyo in Japan. The terrorist can also be a white supremacist or a Maoist for whom power flows from the barrel of a gun . . . it doesn't serve to put a religious or an ethnic face to terror".[22] For a secular democratic nation like India, the external assault may not always be exclusively Islamic. It is sectarianism and religious expansionism in the form of induced and forced conversions; this assault takes as many forms, but the end effect is to raise the dust, and never to give up. These forces are very keen that India remains 'secular' so that they can debunk the spiritual fervour and reduce *Sanatana Dharma* into communal extremism.

The modernization of terrorism is being demonstrated by state-of-the-art methods in the fields of digitization, communication and religious fundamentalism at the turn of the century. Modernization of the defence and police forces, though necessary, is not adequate to meet the challenge of religious crusades. Infiltration from Bangladesh is projected as a serious threat, as also left wing extremism that spans India and Nepal. The secessionist movements in the North East, with influences from far beyond the national boundaries do not any more mark the "external" threats, but indeed constitute a continuum between the external and the internal. Chinese moves to encroach into Arunachal Pradesh, the migrants from Bangladesh as the soft swarm of Jihad, the Maoist-backed Nepali workers and the ULFA are like dormant volcanoes, forming some of the serious 'external' threats to India on the North East front.

Thanks to the globalization of democracy, liberalization of economies and melting of national/cultural borders, incomplete and imperfect as they are, herald a global society sans a global ethic. Terrorism, extremism and fundamentalism are demonstrating a greater degree of cohesion, global linkages and objectives; the nation-states have yet to recognize and evolve a 'global ethic'. A global society cannot operate without a global ethic. India, instead of waiting for such a global ethic to emerge, has to initiate, shape and operationalize such an ethic. In order to be able to do that, India has to develop and sustain a unified vision as a nation.

Policies, Strategies and Actions

In the realm of complex processes of public policy formulation, strategies for the formulation and pursuit of policy, and action to translate policy into changes in the ground-conditions of society, an indicative framework as outlined in illustration 8 can be delineated in order to facilitate a holistic appreciation of the nuances of public policy and management of security in India.

The federal, pluralist polity that is India, with its multi-party system characterized by national, regional and sectarian agenda, the nature of 'politicization' of issues, the diverse hues of colouration as a part of the process of media discourse, the participation of the professional leadership in shaping security policy, the legislative 'by-pass' in the debates on security issues and policy (both in an national and state level legislatures), an administration more fragmented than the polity with antagonistic if not confrontationist dispositions between the union and states, between states, between ministries, between departments, between the (top-down bureaucratic) secretariat and the field offices, and

Phase	*Interactive Institutions*	*Process*	*Modus*
1	Society/Polity	Articulation of Issue / opinion / Interests	Group discourse Public hearing Power of people
2	Political parties	'Politicization' Manifesto : Mandate	Internal debate Public interaction Public education
3	Media/ Professional groups	Public Debate, People's Mandate Public discourse	Participation (in shaping policy)
4	Administration	Feasibility Operational clarity	Role-Goal clarity Cost-Benefit Analyses
5	Legislature	Union-State consultation Legislative framework Resource Allocation	Target setting Prioritization
6	Judicial Dicta	Integration Validation Constitutional vision	Rule of Law Equity : Equality
7	Political Executive Administration	Management of Change	Physical target setting Monitoring, Feed Back Course correction
8	Society	Impact Analyses Results Contra-indicators Consequences	Social Audit Review & Evaluation Feedback

Illustration 8: Indicative Policy Loop in the Constitutional Democratic Frame

most important of all, the hostile dispositions between public administration and the public, influence and often distort the policy formulation and management, turning it into a quagmire. That the administration itself has not 'changed' inspite of a hundred initiatives at the national level alone, towards reform to perform, have not led to any positive impact, testifies to the fact that policy in regard to security remains a quagmire. In the context of a consensual democracy with a national agenda turning into a confrontationist polity where the political parties, national as well as regional, numbering more than 700, preoccupied with capturing power as their prime avocation, the policy process suffers in myriad ways. This distortion is vividly illustrated in regard to the definition (or, redefinition) ascribed to the concept of 'politicization'. Politicization means, the very process of political parties taking note of 'issues' thrown up by the polity, discussing 'internally', interact with the public so as to shape public opinion while at the same time shaping their own electoral manifesto for securing a mandate in favour of their respective policies and programmes. The political parties have a critical role in educating the public and in shaping public opinion on issues and a possible line of action in the best interest of the public, in consonance with the constitutional vision and democratic tradition. In the Indian context, it was Gandhi who said that democracy should not be interpreted as a numerical majority but as *Sarva Jana Hitaaya*. Thus, politicization connotes harmonization, *Samanvaya* as the vital force and process of democracy. But in the Indian context, the political parties, all of them uniformly, have come to conceive and project 'politicization' as subjecting issues of public policy to partisan dispositions and to the pursuit of power; with the 'death' of ideology, pursuit of 'power' has acquired exclusivity.

The 'freedom movement' in India (1847-1947) has lent a distinctly different meaning and substance to 'political' liberation from alien rule. Representing a confluence of values, ideals and ideological moorings, the diverse strands of 'freedom' were woven into the fabric of democracy in India. For Indians, it was '*Sampoorna Swaraj*', freedom in all its splendour – political, economic, social and cultural. The agenda for such a social transformation was set out in the Constitution of India, which constitutes the fountainhead of public policy. The distinctive flavour of the advent of democracy in India was that it was consensual. Three hundred and forty eight elected representatives met for 141 days, and set out the Constitution, spread over 395 Articles. Credit goes to the leadership, the quality of leadership.

As a historical parallel, for the first time in the history of human society, a set of rights and freedoms was affirmed for all people everywhere in the form and title of the Universal Declaration of

Human Rights, on Dec. 10, 1948. About the same time the Constituent Assembly of India had contextualized the most comprehensive 'universal human rights' (encompassing the political, economic, social and cultural freedoms) and adopted them as Fundamental Rights on 26th Nov., 1949. It deserves and demands reiteration that the objectives resolution was introduced by Jawaharlal Nehru in the first session of the Constituent Assembly thus:

"In this Constituent Assembly, we are functioning on a world stage and the eyes of the world are upon us and the eyes of our entire past are upon us. Our past is witness to what we are doing here and though the future is still unborn, the future too somehow looks at us. I beg to move:

1. This Constituent Assembly declares it from and solemn resolve to proclaim India as an *Independent Sovereign Republic* and to draw up for her future governance a Constitution;
2. Wherein the said territories, whether with their present boundaries or with such others as may be determined by the Constituent Assembly and thereafter according to the Law of the Constitution, shall possess and retain the status of *autonomous units*, together with residuary powers, and exercise all powers and functions of government and administration, save and except such powers and functions as are vested in or assigned to the Union, or as are inherent or implied in the Union or resulting there from; and
3. Wherein *all powers and authority* of the Sovereign Independent India, its constituent parts and organs of government, are derived from the people; and
4. Wherein shall be *guaranteed and secured to all the people of India* justice, social, economic and political: equality of status, of opportunity, and before the law: freedom of thought, expression, belief. faith, worship, vocation, association and action, subject to law and public morality; and
5. Wherein *adequate safeguards* shall be provided for

minorities, backward and tribal areas and depressed and other backward classes; and

6. Whereby shall be maintained the *integrity of the territory* of the Republic and its sovereign rights on land, sea, and air according to justice and the law of civilized nations, and
7. This ancient land attains its rightful and honoured place in the world and make its *full and willing contribution to the promotion of world peace* and the welfare of mankind".

The Constitution of India is not a mere rule book of India's constitutional governance. It sets out a national agenda, a charter for total social transformation. The Constitution has clearly pronounced a 'Union of States' with a few federal features, India's constitution is sculpted, adapted and adopted in the name, and on behalf of the people of India.

The roles and responsibilities between the union and the states have been delineated in terms of Union List, State List and Concurrent List. Under the Constitution the boundaries of states can be altered, new states carved out, existing states can be merged, including their names, by the Union.

Within these constitutional parameters, states have been assigned the responsibility of maintaining *inter alia*, 'Law and Order'. Yet, it is not an exclusive responsibility of the states as the Union has been assigned the overall responsibility of the nation's security.

Under Articles 355 and 356 of the Constitution, the Union can supersede the popular government in the states, proclaim Presidents' Rule in any state on grounds of law and order, peace and constitutional governance, due to either external and / or internal threats. There is no confusion about the overarching role and responsibility of the Union in regard to the maintenance of law and social order. The first six decades of constitutional democracy have witnessed, on about 400 occasions, this higher-order responsibility assumed by the Union. The Union has also set up a number of Central Police Organizations (CPOs) and Para-Military Forces (PMFs) apart from intelligence and investigation agencies such as the Intelligence Bureau (IB), the Central Bureau of Investigation (CBI). Ministry of Home Affairs (MHA) of the Government of India (GOI) has assumed the role of managing and sustaining internal security and law and order.

One of the paradoxes is that though the democratic constitution has been proclaimed on the 26th January 1950, the Police Act 1861 framed by the alien rulers, with the prime objective of protecting their proprietary 'rights', 'trade' and adjunct interests, is yet to be tuned to the demands of India's constitutional democracy. Even the cardinal recommendations of the National Police Commission set up by the Government of India which had submitted its recommendations were debated and well endorsed by the people, nationwide, have not been adopted and translated into action by the political executive. The Supreme Court has decreed, twice, for the setting up, on a permanent basis, of a National Security Commission and State Security Commissions at the level of states, with the aim of focusing on security management, and protecting the police and their performance from possible partisan political impingement, and to ensure accountability of police to the law of the land, and these to the people of India. Almost all the political parties, while in power, have shown their reluctance to the idea, uniformly and consistently. Almost all the parties have been in power, some time, in some state or the other. While in power, they did not themselves act on the Supreme Court's Judgement, and yet while in the opposition, all the political parties consistently criticize the party in power, of misuse and abuse of police under Article 356 of the Constitution. It is this dichotomy or duality in the pursuit of policy that has led to public interest litigation (PIL) two times; on both the occasions the opinion of the highest court of the land was defied; deadlines set by the Court for action have been ignored, by all the political parties.

The constitution has been amended almost a hundred times in the first six decades. In a centralized constitutional regime, the 73rd and 74th amendments were aimed at decentralization of the administrative structures of governance and promotion of the people's participation in the direction of participative democracy and development. The third tier institutions of governance, popularly referred to as the *Panchayati Raj* institutions (PRIs), encompassed the District level (*Zilla Parishad, Mandal* and village level) institutions of 'grass-root' democracy. Under this decentralized constitutional scheme, 29 items were culled out from the Union, State and the Concurrent Lists of the Constitution and assigned to the *Panchayati Raj* Institutions.

Under the scheme of decentralization, 'policing' was debated, as an appropriate item for 'decentralization'. In fact it was so provided in the statute in the state of Karnataka, but quickly retreated. The police was excluded from the participative, as well as consultative process at the district level governance. On the other hand, Members of Parliament (MPs) and of the state legislatures (MLAs) were made, ex-officio Members of the respective *Zilla Parishads* and MLAs as Members of the *Mandal Parishads*, knowing that such a provision could prove to be a fifth wheel. On the ground, as a matter of fact, the constitutional amendments 73rd and 74th proclaiming decentralized structures have witnessed hierarchical, centralized, bureaucratic structures were left intact; the amendments have only witnessed an unprecedented political 're-centralization'. Members of Parliament and of state legislatures with their ex-officio membership of *Panchayati Raj* Institutions are also authorized discretionary Constituency and Local Area Development Funds to the tune of Rs. 2 to 5 crores. The Comptroller and Auditor General (CAG) of India has observed, repeatedly, that these funds are the most abused, leading to corrupt practices, on an extensive scale. To mock such decentralization, state-level Election Commissions and Finance Commissions have been set up. On the ground PRIs had always been starved of funds; they were put on a starvation diet.

Police organizations have been (a) kept aloof, untouched by the process of *de-jure* decentralization; and (b) even community-policing in any of its mutations has not been innovated much less put in place. On the other hand, the higher order, upper levels of the police organizations have been allowed to bulge in the form of zonal/regional/intermediate IGs/DIGs/ et al. Even more, there has been an extensive proliferation of specialized branches within each of the police organizations, at the centre, not to speak of specialized organizations within each state. With such a proliferation and lack of measurable standards and measures for their performance, there has emerged a hierarchy within the police organizations. There has also been an enormous growth of numbers in terms of battalions. The much debated 'community policing' not only as a part of decentralized, participative process, but also from the standpoint of efficiencies and effectiveness, has not taken place. Police-Public cooperation remains a euphemism on paper. Police desire public cooperation, with the premise that without public cooperation the police cannot be effective. There has not been any argument about the need for and desirability of police cooperating with the public. There is not much of synergy among the various police organizations, either.

There have been repeated consultative processes between the union and the states on issues of policing and police organizational management. At the apex level, apart from a cabinet sub-committee on security, there have been periodic conferences of Governors, of Chief Ministers, of Home Ministers, of Directors General of Police, et al – either on an annual basis, or on an ad hoc or emergency basis, as and when specific issues, such as left wing extremism, human rights abuses, custodial crimes, atrocities against vulnerable sections of the society, prison reforms, training on human rights, inter-state coordination and cooperation, need to strengthen anti-terror legislation have cropped up.

Given the multi-party system, pluralist multi-cultural society we live in – described as a place where three centuries coexist as a parallel—these interactions, at several levels, between the Union and the states as well as between states, have not yielded the desired measure of results in terms of police performance and management of police. Nothing illustrates the contradictions or distortions that creep into these interactions as the infructuous national debate on Prevention of Terrorism Act, 2002 (POTA); the need for a federal agency to meet the challenge of terrorism spanning across the boundaries of states, sharing of intelligence (in order to be able to meet the single serious threat to national security) which is a *sine qua non* to improve the operational efficacy and effectiveness of all forces together.

All the reform panels on police, policing, and police organizations, as also a series of both 'high-power' and 'high-level' expert committees and commissions commending enactment of a strong law to fight terrorism has only yielded partisan political debate both within and outside the Parliament. All party meets to discuss terrorism also ended up as tea parties. Chief Ministers' conclaves – a healthy practice of consensual democracy—also endorsed, time and again, strong action only to end up as a whimper without any concrete follow-up action. The seriousness of the issue of terrorism was only matched by grandiose declarations and frivolous actions.

All the Prime Ministers heading different parties or coalition governments have publicly emphasized, all the time, the need for strengthening anti-terror laws. When the Bharatiya Janata Party led National Democratic Alliance introduced Prevention of Terrorism Act (POTA), in the wake of a series of terrorist attacks, including the *Akshardham* and Parliament House, it was opposed tooth and nail, both inside and outside the Parliament on grounds that such a legislation would be misread and abused, and that it may be targeted against one community. The need for and merit of the law *per se* was not questioned. No safeguards were proposed as amendments so as to prevent apprehended abuse. No objections were raised on ideological grounds either. And when there was a change of guard, from the NDA to the United Progressive Alliance (UPA) led by the Indian National Congress Party, POTA was abrogated with a measure of urgency, without bringing in any alternative legislation. It was a classic situation in India's democratic history that in the wake of a long series of terrorist attacks, the political debate only attained an ever increasingly higher pitch, all focused on the POTA, as if POTA represented a political prototype. It was also strange to witness senior members of the cabinet making such frivolous statements as "POTA has failed to stop terror"; POTA was opposed, instead of making it effective and strong. It was the 10-member-strong terrorists who travelled by a hijacked boat and landed at the Gateway of India and attacked half a dozen prominent and strategic locations in Mumbai that prompted Indian democracy to wake up, bring into existence an anti-terror legislation with an all-India reach without any debate on possible misuse, or potential abuse. The Pak terrorists did not violate any anti-terror law either, for such a law only followed the royal entry of terrorists and shocking terrorist destruction spread over more than three days, non-stop. India's media too, perhaps unwillingly, but may be unthinkingly, facilitated the terrorists in their operations. It was a shame on Indian democracy that we had a fierce and prolonged debate and conceived a paper but had not produced an effective anti-terror law in 20 long years. The Union Home Minister had presented a concept paper on terrorism, internal security and action plans, to tackle the newly emerging metro-terrorism. The valiant police forces had demonstrated their dedication and devotion in tackling terrorism, and the voice of demos sent the Union Home Minister packing.

The same pattern and phenomenon was exhibited in the debate on the 'need' for a federal investigation agency to probe inter-state and trans-border crimes, including acts of terrorism. This proposal came up for discussion in the face of mounting evidence of terrorists operating from some centres, states and cities, as safe-havens, indulging in acts of terrorism in other states. The Ruling and the Opposition divide in such debates was as clear as daylight. The dialogues on internal security went on in the manner of fire crackers played at marriage parties, not on the lines of concern for national security in the face of an onslaught on our nation and its integrity.

Increasing the ratio of police to population, imparting training to face new challenges, modernization of police forces, strengthening of intelligence gathering and sharing mechanisms incrementally, and earmarking more funds for matters relating to security have been the standard pills for all the critical ills of national security. Vote banks constituted a 'constant' concern. Vote bank politics had always dominated the centre-state, inter-state, and multi-party cooperation. Several state governments had refused to cooperate in anti-terrorist operations for fear of communal tensions, i.e. fear of loss of votes. Where is the chance to seriously, and candidly discuss the dispositions of regional parties on issues of national security and integrity where the survival of national governments was entirely dependent on 'alliance dharma' with the regional and sectarian political outfits?

The Foreigners Act 1946, and tribunals set up under the Act represent another classic case of compromising public safety as well as national interest as a consequence of the pursuit of vote bank politics. The pursuit of power at any cost and retaining it at all costs has become the bane of 'democracy' in India. Even death sentences awarded by the Supreme Court of India for committing a heinous crime such as an attack on the Indian Parliament has been 'set aside' by the largest democracy, wanting to become the greatest.

The Supreme Court stayed the orders of the Special Tribunal, quashing a notification declaring the Students Islamic Movement of India (SIMI) an unlawful organization under the Unlawful Activities (Prevention) Act 1967. The Bench ordered notice to the SIMI seeking its response in three weeks. The Attorney General submitted that the Tribunal in its 264-page order did not express on the merits of the case though the Government had provided Intelligence Bureau reports pointing to the involvement of SIMI members in terrorist activities. He said the Tribunal had done something above the law and order and if the Order was not stayed, it would result in serious consequences. The Centre observed that "being a group of students and youth, the SIMI is easily influenced by hardcore Muslim terrorist organizations operating from Jammu and Kashmir. The Hizbul Mujahideen and the Lashkar–e–Taiba have successfully penetrated into SIMI cadre to achieve their goals." It was also stated that the SIMI had launched a countrywide campaign, since November 1996, to mobilize support for Muslims and a caliphate for the community. The SIMI was against Indian nationalism and worked to replace it with an international Islamic order. The organization was active in Andhra Pradesh, Assam, Bihar, Gujarat, Karnataka, Kerala, Tamil Nadu, Jharkhand, Madhya Pradesh, Maharashtra, Rajasthan, Uttar Pradesh, West Bengal and the National Capital Territory of Delhi.

Referring to the Tribunal's finding that the notification did not specify the reason for declaring the SIMI an unlawful association, the SLP said, "It had failed to take into consideration voluminous oral and documentary evidence justifying the ban". It was brought to the Tribunal's notice that the draft notification was attached to a Cabinet note, which was presented in a sealed cover.

The Centre said, "It was clearly mentioned in the notification that if the SIMI's unlawful activities were not curbed immediately, it would continue with its subversive activities and reorganize its activists who were still absconding, destroy the secular fabric of the country, polluting the minds of the people by creating communal disharmony, propagate anti-national sentiments and escalate secessionism by supporting militancy".[23]

The Foreigners' Act 1946 provided for detection of and strict punishment to infiltrators considering that a large number of them came from neighbouring countries, including East and West Pakistan. The Supreme Court held that there is a need for imposing a stricter sentence under the Foreigners Act. But, the political leadership continues to demonstrate that India remains a soft state, in perpetuity. Who else can say: "thus far and no further" in matters of national security and integrity?

Naxalism[24] has been yet another classic case of the consequence of distortions that have crept into the process of socio-economic development. A case of marginalization, deprivation, and alienation as a direct consequence of faulted and failed socio-legal engineering, and corruption that has spread into the body politic of democratic India. Naxal, left-wing or social activist leadership emerges wherever and whenever there is a social and political vacuum. Wherever and whenever any movement emerges and operates for a long time, such a movement itself gets corrupted. That is what has precisely happened – socio-economic distortions have germinated conflict which turned into Naxalism – picking up selective agenda and tactics, shifting and changing the agenda and tactics and spreading its arena like a chameleon. The diverse mutations of Naxalism are treated as a single phenomenon. It was never discussed in the national and state legislatures as a part of the democratic political process, but subjected to partisan considerations, pressures and interests in the ever-changing political scenario. On many an occasion, political parties had been seen pursuing and abusing the Naxal issues for partisan gains

Debate on this phenomenon was made complex and frivolous, giving way, over a period of time, into pseudo-Naxalism, mere lawless groups operating with impunity as Naxalite groups. Such phenomenon was natural when a movement like Naxalism has spread over several states, with strategic alliances between terrorist outfits within, and cross-border extremist organizations seeking landing sites and shades of 'legitimacy'. Compared to the complexity and spread of Naxalism, which continues to grow, perhaps the core issue has been pushed to the periphery in the process of policy formulation in India. The phenomenon of Naxalism came handy for political parties to play the blame-game. There have been feeble and occasional discussions in the resolution of conflict; such efforts in peace-making have never been seen as earnest, sustained or consistent.

In India's constitutional democracy, innovation has been explored and established in the direction of extra-constitutional and anti-democratic modes, untouched by the canvas of rule of law and transparency in governance. This was vivdly illustrated in the case of *Salwa Judum*, arousing the citizens against fellow citizens (called Naxalites) first, and when the State of Chhattisgarh had found that *Salwa Judum* rebounded on the State, it had innovated yet another unconstitutional and equally anti-democratic idea of Koya commandos.

"53 years after our independence there is no clear understanding among our leaders, our political class, our bureaucracy, business establishment and intellectuals about the nature of the security problems India faces..........It would appear that one of the most difficult challenges to Indian security we face is the general indifference to security on the part of our elite," observed K. Subrahmanyam.[25]

How far and how well, can the militant streams, such as Maoists and Naxals in India, be drawn back into the mainstream? How long would it take and what would be the historical hangovers of such mainstreaming? Experience has shown that many such episodes had left a bitter taste in that the 'deviants' were not allowed to get absorbed by the extremists themselves; those who preferred to get back to the mainstream were dubbed as informers and finished. The general population had often been seen wondering if there was a genuine change of heart; plans for creating special battalions of former Naxals, and of tribals, to fight the 'Naxals' was met with a public hue and cry on the grounds that such measures would not only be counter-productive but could in fact, escalate the levels of conflict.

Several announcements at addressing the basic issues of development and mainstreaming of people in the backward areas continue to be mere pious declarations for public consumption, in the face of continuing and mounting distortions creeping into the life of people in the backward areas. Some innovative initiatives like Remote and Interior Areas Development (RIAD) as in Andhra Pradesh are reduced to mere paper programmes. Development of backward areas has been reduced to the grounding of certain large-scale industrial, infrastructural, and/or irrigation projects but not tuned to make them relevant to the people in 'backward' areas. As the people are not 'mainstreamed' into the development process, they continue to slide into marginalization and deprivation, not just exclusion from the process of development. Mainstreaming people has yet to be adequately appreciated and operationalized as an integral part of the process of development. It is this failure, that is reflected in terms of degradation of the lives of the poor, in terms of the alarming slide in Human Development Indices (HDI), that is directly contributing to the Gross Social Conflict (GSC) in India.

In India's democracy, the administrative (personnel, and thus the) system had operated, for long, within an ambience of exclusivity, confidentiality and secrecy. The Gandhian tenet of keeping windows and doors open, while standing firm on the ground allowing the fresh breeze of thought, had no impact. Thanks to the institutions that had extended huge developmental funding with an in-built component for consulting, and study tours abroad, the bureaucratic barriers are not only melting, but have also started to fan out as "consultants". However, this happy turn has yet to translate into their contribution as change agents at home, especially in the field of public policy formulation and management.

The policy process itself demonstrates many more distortions such as (a) police which was seen as an instrument of promoting, sustaining harmony, as a peace force in the democratic republic, had remained a *lathi-force*, operating outside the ethos of 'planned' development. The pantheon of police organizations themselves seem to operate in isolation of each other, within a culture of hierarchical status matched at each level, by a culture of "decentralization upto me", but "centralization below me". Police have grown into large and complex organizations but without adequate mechanisms of 'strategic think tanks' within. There are such units, by design, such as the Bureau of Police Research and Development, (BPR&D) and the National Crime Records Bureau, (NCRB) that brings out an annual document of statistics on crime. There has not been adequate churning on policing issues and strategic approaches within the police organizations even in the apex training academies. What the police themselves can do in terms of an initiative to contain and reverse the antagonism and hostile relations as between the police and the public is to assume a role (if not the role) of establishing alliances with the institutions of civil society, and actively promoting human rights education, adopting a campaign mode. Police organizations, like the Police Science Congress, could take a more active role in articulating on issues of national security policy, and help shape public policy with their inputs rather than accept the 'policy' as 'given' by the distorted democratic process. Promoting their own professional image would also lead to the higher judiciary 'respecting' the police as a credible organization rather than passing strictures so often with an ever-increasing tendency to control, direct and monitor the professional performance of police. By assuming an "open dialogue", police can perform their professional role and thus strengthen their efficacy and effectiveness, leading to a positive image and enhanced credibility.

Political as well as police leadership appear to be at its wits end, groping for policy initiatives, options, choices and implications of the options available. The situation is made complex because in the absence of a holistic and consensual appreciation of the problems and issues, political opinion reflects its own partisan divergence, with the union and states pursuing policy in isolation. As the problem of left wing extremism continues to grow in its complexity, party leadership prescribes soft options on the premise that elimination of individuals cannot be a solution. But the leadership in power takes a position that there is no other option but state power to contain Maoist actions of subversion and violence. The Union Government, somewhat far away from the impact zones of armed conflict initiates outreach programmes to promote awareness regarding government policies and programmes, such as Bharat Nirman, RTI, NRHM and MGNREGA.

It is recognized at the policy level, and declared, both at home and abroad that terrorism has to be fought across all fronts and that Maoist violence has to be pursued in a spirit of conflict resolution. It is recognized that if people had legitimate sources of earning a livelihood, they would be less likely to work for $10 a day for Taliban in Afghanistan. But, policies are tested on the ground, not merely in terms of strategies, their adequacy, appropriateness, impact and consequences.

The intervening problems that emerge in the pursuit of policy – such as *Salwa Judum*, The Armed Forces Special Powers Act, Police excesses increasingly being taken (occasionally *suo motu*) cognizance of by the Judiciary, governments' responsibility in regard to destruction of life and property in the name of Bandhs, deployment of central forces in the states, political partisan pressures skewing terror investigations, emerge to the fore as a few of the many nuances of strategies.

3

Police at the Cross Roads: Stress and Strain

At the time of the beginning of India's freedom movement (1857), under those mutinous conditions, the Police Act 1861 was enacted by the British – to shape the police as an instrument of subjugation and coercion of the 'subjects'. The singular objective was to retain 'control', with or without suppressive methods. Police were used as an instrument for enslaving people as subjects. A century of conditioning, and internalization of this ethos by the police were sustained by the alien rulers. Subjugation of the people constituted the measure of effective performance by the police. There was no chance for any accountability to people, or 'professionalism' of the police; they were not factored.

Then came democratic freedom and the challenge of managing freedom, liberty of the subjugated people who had turned into sovereign citizens of the constitutional Republic. The transition, especially for the police, amounted to an awkward and jerky U-turn. But a statesman Sardar Vallabhbhai Patel, titled the 'iron-man' was in command as the first Home Minister of India. He lent substantive meaning to democracy and national discipline, so he could impart clarity of purpose and set the social sights for the police. The police ethos and organizational mission he had set out was crystallized into a modicum of organizational culture. He encouraged organizational role clarity, stability, and performance with accountability. Thus, until 1965, the Inspector General (as the heads of Police were then designated) stayed in office, with a clear line of command, undisturbed, for periods ranging from 8 to 12 years. By 1980-85 the police chiefs, re-designated, upgraded and multiplied as Directors General had an average tenure of 6 to 12 months; the Station House Officer (SHO) today is posted and operates at the pleasure of the local Member of the Legislative Assembly (MLA). This was only one of the impacts, consequences, to be precise, of political transition on police organizations. Constitutionally, we the people have chosen to have the rule of law as a cardinal characteristic of our democracy. Instead of redefining the role and redesigning the organization our prime movers i.e., political executives and bosses have ushered in de facto control and (mis)management of the police.

Political Transition

Context and Content

It is a historical paradox that right through several centuries, India has lost territory; and, almost as a parallel, every territorial loss was followed by an enhanced threat to its internal security. Such threats emerging from its own lost territory, truly made a continuum of the external and internal dimensions of the security scenario. It is recorded history[26] that has left an imprint as a historical memory. Over the millennia, the territorial expanse of India *Akhand Bharat* was recorded as 70,40,700 square kilometers. As of 15th August, 1947, India won its struggle with the British, but territorially, Bharat has lost 56 per cent, of its land mass and the leftover 44 per cent is called India i.e. Bharat, not "Bharat i.e. India".

India today is the 7th largest country, with the second largest population – of over a billion (as of 2005). Apart from 600 island territories, its borders consist of 15,800 km. of land, 7,683 km of coast line, 25 sq. km. of exclusive economic zone. It has common land borders with six nations and maritime boundaries with five nations. While the land boundaries have remained porous for decades, the year 2008 had conclusively found that the coastal boundaries were left unattended, and it proved disastrous during November 2008, to our national security and integrity. Some of our island territories are closer to our neighbours than to our own mainland. India has never added even one square kilometer to its territory.

Historically, the structures of power and authority in society were founded on factors such as the legitimacy of benign monarchies, or military might, colonial or dictatorial. In effect, the structures of authority, public institutions as well as private organizations, had achieved and sustained the cooperation and compliance of the public in order to be able to meet the criteria of legitimacy and credibility to varying degrees. In the process, people were habituated to complying with the directives issued by the authorities contributing to the reinforcement of institutional authority and the leadership process. But, in contemporary times of democracy, in the brief spell of six decades, power and authority have shifted from the structures of state to the people not on the basis of normative policy initiatives such as administrative decentralization and people's participation but, as a consequence of malfunctioning of the institutions of state in addressing and upholding organizational goals, and standards of performance. The erosion of authority is symbolized by "people taking law into their hands" representing trends of anarchy, reinforcing the acronym of a "functional anarchy". In the ever-changing mainstream of democracy globally, it is logical that there emerge cross currents such as extremism at one end, and civil liberties and pressure groups on the other, seeking to educate, empower, and thus help people participate as partners in democracy. Fragmentation of political organizations as well as the leadership, manifest in India is a direct consequence of distortions of power.

Under the democratic disposition, police leadership have not yet come to prepare their organizations appropriately and adequately, to recognize and establish partnerships and democratic equations with the citizens. There are also police officers who look at civil society organizations as 'adversaries'. As a consequence of the pervasive crises of authority, states and governments have become less effective in confronting challenges and implementing policies. They have come to maintain public order through 'police power', but their ability to address and solve substantive issues is declining rather alarmingly. People withhold 'cooperation', which is a vital prerequisite for legitimacy and credible performance of the institutions of state.

Deviation from established norms, conventions and rules without adequate justification for such deviation, destabilize the 'game' of democracy. Rules are as important, if not more, as the game of democracy. If such 'rules' are changed, ignored, deviated from, without an explicitly stated rationale it amounts to partisan 'politicization' of the game. Politicization in the positive sense of bringing issues into the realm of legitimacy through dialogue and public debate is almost absent. Projecting and adjudging issues from the stand point of the 'partisan' is leading to 'malignancy' of the political process itself in India's democracy.

In the 2008 edition of its Annual Democracy Index, *The Economist* placed India among the 50 countries found to be "flawed democracies'. The various political parties, based on sectarian values and partisan identities do not contribute to the management of a democratic polity; their mode of management is reduced to pitting people against people. Confrontation and hostility characterize the relations between the various political organizations. Conflict is the 'dominant mode' of their operating India's democratic polity, with the attendant consequence of social conflict and violence which is a contra-indicator of democracy. Criminals are sponsored by political parties, and find their place in the legislatures.

Marshals are summoned with increasing frequency, with the result that the legislative flares lead to street corner flash points. Instead of the legislatures discussing peoples' problems, people are left debating the challenge of political malignancies like vote bank politics. Peoples' distress with political leaders is channeled into disdain for democratic values.

"Criminalization of politics is a clear sign of the breakdown of the existing system; it signals the advent of mobocracy".[27] Criminalization of politics and politicization of crime have encircled India's democracy, during the early (formative) decades of its emergence, and long before the advent of the 21st century. Violence of all shades has been so absorbed into the mainstream of political process, encompassing both 'ruling' and 'opposition' parties, including intra-party politics, to such an extent that India has assumed the character of a violent democracy. Not for nothing is India categorized as among the 50 flawed democracies in the comity of nations.

Left Wing Extremism had emerged due to an extensive range of distortions of socio-economic development.[28] Yet the issue was never discussed or debated within the legislatures in search of a democratically sustainable consensual solution.

India's ideal of secularism has emerged as a debauched variant, leading to a perverted mutation of naked communalism and "communal" divide. There is a political force behind every conflict that is labeled "communal". Communal divide has come in handy for the leaders of Indian democracy, so they can divide, and rule like the British did. In the case of this home-made brew, it is 'divide', abuse and 'misrule'.

Terrorism is yet another spice in India's democracy. Any and every terror discourse is not focused on the alternative modes or methods of containing, but gets blocked by centre-state or ruling versus opposition malignancies. The political will does not match the will and skill of terrorists. Democracy and development, and deficiencies in the process of governance are caught in the maelstrom of conflict; India's political process has yet to grasp and learn to manage conflict. There is a federal trauma affecting Indian democracy, with a flurry of myriad conferences both at political and administrative levels. Suddenly, terrorist issues are clouded by the dynamics of federal nuances, and states expressing reservations against central 'encroachments' on their legislative or administrative 'autonomy'.

In the face of externally induced internal threats, fundamentalism, organized crime, disruption of public order, cyber crimes, money laundering, drugs and arms, extremism, terrorism, insurgency, militancy and secessionism constitute one set of threats, while conflict of values of a pluralist polity, communal and caste wars, sectarianism, regionalism and ethnicity constitute the other set. While it is recognized that good policing as a part of good governance is the bedrock of a sound national strategy for security, competitive populism and partisan politics of power have accentuated the threat perceptions to the democratic order in India. It is in this canvas that critical questions about efficiency and effectiveness of police organizations emerge to the fore.

Liberal budgetary support, creation and expansion of Central Police Organizations and Para Military Forces, including rapid creation of the Rapid Action Force, and anti-terrorist units on an emergency basis, continued army assistance even in civil disturbances, emergencies, and disaster situations, had proved to be some of the political responses to the emerging security scenario. CBI's assistance—in what may be called 'political emergencies' aimed at buying time and staving off the onslaught of 'opposition' parties and public indignation—has, for long, been used as a rescue force in political emergencies.

The ever accentuating debate, often acrimonious, on a strong centre versus strong states reveals the unsettled status and unsettling state of the federal equations in India. The several diverse and mutually conflicting argu/ments on the issue focus more on the structure and authority of government and political culture rather than on concern for national integrity and integration. The founding fathers of the nation debated the issue in the context of the traumatic partition of the country and the hatred and bloodshed that had followed. Our contemporary democratic political process has not been able to restore any semblance of 'normany', but in fact tended to internalize into the body politic the factors that had prevailed and created a 'divide' in society. In this vitiated political environment the several and ever expanding central and state police forces have not developed synergies in operation even in the face of several affronts to the nation's democratic character, and the combined image of the police forces.

The political environment within which the police have been functioning is reflected in the growing and widespread political partisan influence and interference in the day-to-day administration and functioning of the police. The objectives set by law for police organizations are at variance with the role and purposes being served by the police in practice. The functional autonomy of the police is also diluted due to lax observance of norms of recruitment, promotion, tenure and 'transfer'. The dominant role that the media plays today, in spreading news and views, has emerged as yet another critical facet of the environment within which the police operate. Whether the police seek to and have succeeded in influencing the environment is debatable: and remains so.

The political ethos characterized by antagonistic dispositions such as 'ruling versus opposition', and 'centre versus state', also influence police organizations and operations in multifarious modes, most often adversely. The 'ruling' party tends to defend the police even as the 'opposition' parties tend to condemn the police. In fact, the police are used as a stick in the eternal fight between political parties. The situation is such that no 'ruling' party tends to disown, much less condemn the police even in known cases of excesses or improprieties. We have been piling archives of commissions – judicial or otherwise – appointed whenever police excesses and/or atrocities are alleged.

The power shift, colonial to constitutional democracy, *de jure* has changed the status of 'subjects' into "we, the people", with the constitutional blueprint designed to transform the people into proud citizens, as sovereign masters, conforming to the discipline of a democracy. There was no 'alien ruler', nor can there be an *alibi* for decades, of an overbearing empire and antiquated law. There has not been any voice from the leadership of police organizations demanding autonomy matching in the constitutional, legal and democratic role and responsibilities. Here again, it is left to the citizens-groups to agitate and demand operational autonomy for the police.

During colonial times, the people were united by a common adversary, the British. But, with their departure, the focal point of unity, which is social transformations, has witnessed bitter fragmentation in the form of a multitude of more than 700 political parties, with a single point agenda viz., political power. Polarization of the people based on a multiplex of factors such as region, language, ethnicity, community, caste, rural-urban, agricultural-industrial, et al. has contributed to conditions of internal strife, labeled with relative ease, as a characteristic of 'pluralism'. In such a state of social strife and disruption, socio-economic developmental efforts are bound to create a backlash of political turbulence and loss of equilibrium. This, in essence, is the state of the Indian polity.

It is in such a social scenario that leadership assumes a critical role and place in shaping the vision of a society in leading it from 'darkness to light'. India had the good fortune of statesmen–like leadership, who gave their all and turned from riches to rags. A historically pluralistic society was united like 'one-man'. As political leaders took over from statesmen, they turned the nascent nation against itself, making people wonder whether Winston Churchill was right in his prediction that India (i.e. its leadership) will fail themselves and together, the nation. In no time, a proud democratic nation was reduced to a 'soft state' and a 'functioning anarchy'. With such leadership, it was logical that the national vision got distorted into a political drama and the enervation of the institutions of state especially the police, leading to social trauma.

A functional anarchy resorts to legislated social order, with legislation as the '*mantra*' for social transformation. What India has witnessed is an avalanche of legislation. The economic canon of 'law of diminishing returns' has reemerged in the manner of 'diminishing returns of law' coupled with a state of legislative 'excess', matched by lawlessness on the ground. If the British had enacted about 400 pieces of legislation in 10 decades, democratic India has enacted more than an estimated 5,000 pieces of legislation in its first five decades.

Citing a few pertinent examples, such as a Commissioner of Police informing the media that "a section of senior police officers refused to be on the ground and take on the terrorists". The fabrication of forensic evidence in politically sensitive cases, the manner in which the issue of a state security commission at the national and state levels and many more, have been handled by the political system, the setting up of a multitude of national as well as state-level commissions on human rights, women's rights, children's rights, et al, represent a political placebo in the management of India's democracy, and police transformation. The distortions in the political democratic ethic of India are innumerable. These distortions have been operating in a cyclical manner; they can't be neatly segregated as either causes or as consequences. Did the police themselves, their leadership in particular, manage to transform the police? If so how?

Police Transformation

Growth and Development

In the face of national harmony getting distorted, the process of harmonization is giving way to national confrontation. Police-maoist confrontation has grown from 'local' levels and has become the numero uno national problem. Organized red-armies (getting ready for Lalgarh) are spreading all over. *Adivasis* are either getting 'hit', or being sucked into insurgencies. Elections are being held subject to the availability of security forces. Continuing communal hatred is a constant, in the manner of a series, right from 1947 through 1984, into the first decade of 21st century. The Indian state, in an adversarial and confrontationist political culture, is debating policy options and legislative measures like the imposition of a ban on some of the parties and front organizations. The police in India is caught-up, in between a liberal democratic polity and anti-democratic forces.

How and how far has the police been transformed in the face of the trauma of political transition? What were the pre-existing modes and methods and demands of change? How far are the nation, the state and the police itself conscious of the changed context and demands of organizational transformation on the Police? A prime reality that appears to emerge is that Indian police organizations, the policeman as well as his leaders, and the systems that they had developed during the period 1861 to 1950, have remained intact largely unmindful of the imperatives and demands of the constitutional culture and democratic transformation.

Clearly, there are methods and modes prevailing in the management of police organizations that are outdated and undemocratic, and now subjected to partisan politics. Proliferation of structures without a role-goal delineation among police organizations, and the unresolved problems of interface management have led to demoralization of all police forces. Police are aware of the deficiencies in their performance that are either explained away, or a new structure is created as a solution. This process of proliferation has led to a hierarchy among police organizations instead of complementarity and convergence in their performance. The CBI which was projected as an ace professional organization has been seen and used as a dustbin to throw in all politically uncomfortable cases so that the central government could assure the chief ministers of states that the proposed new federal agency "would not function like the CBI". In the wake of the Mumbai terror attack (26/11/2008), the Union Home Minister had reiterated the obvious: "We will attempt to change the way policing is done", in the country.

We do not need to waste time in analyzing and identifying what is needed to be done. Several eminent persons and national and state level commissions, not to speak of the Supreme Court and several High Courts have carved out the fundamental requisites of police transformation. As the Home Minister said, "We don't need any 'white paper', or whitewash but 'action'". He seems to be stating that now the police transformation is backed up by political will. The police cannot perhaps any more maintain the absence of 'political will' as an alibi for either under- or non-performance. If the police are to protect and sustain the democratic order, they need to cultivate their administrative will in order to transform their organizations to meet the demands of a democratizing polity. At the point of political freedom, where was the police? What has been the agenda, of the police if any, in the context of the sea-change of democratization of Indian society, and social transformation as an ongoing process? What is the police response to the demands of a democratizing society?

The role of the police has changed since India became a constitutional democracy, but its role has not been redefined, either *de jure*, or *de facto* with the consequence that the basic architecture and functional ethos have remained static, and thus outdated, without being adequately and consciously attuned to a democratizing society. The demands on the police organizations have kept on growing, almost constantly and largely with non-policing roles. Tasks that legitimately and logically do not belong to police have been loaded onto the police, not merely because other organizations so 'manoeuvered it', but the mainline police organizations had never objected to such *ad hoc* and 'indiscriminate' overload. May be some such non-policing roles had adversely changed the character of police organizations, but the way of policing had been shaped by accident or chance, rather than by design. With an expansion in the core policing role of maintaining law and order, with both quantitative as well as qualitative expansion in the nature, range and volume of crime, the demands of crime control and of the criminal justice system on the police have grown by leaps as the 'recorded' data reveal. If the "non-recorded" or non-registered cases, to be more precise, are also taken into consideration, the issue gets more complex. The expanding role and load, far beyond crime control, and law and order, has led to an expansion of police strength both at the national and state levels. The nature of growth can be profiled in a static overview. The nature, pattern and categories of crime in India, alongside the emergence of new categories of crime, as of 2008, presented in Table 1 is noteworthy.

The political parties, have proved that in a situation of competitive populism and pursuit of power *per se*, democracy suffers several and severe distortions, such as democracy turning violent, as it happened in India. It is essentially a consequence of the distortions in the management of the electoral process and economic growth in a manner that would subserve social transformation. The turbulence and turmoil caused by these enormous distortions of development have been dredged to the doorsteps of the police. It is not of their making, nor can they be expected, legitimately, to resolve such complex problems where the political, the economic and the social factors interplay and consequently operate concurrently. Such distortions, when allowed to operate in a sustained manner over a period of time, grow more complex, become difficult even for the political system to manage. In the contemporary history of India, the unintended consequences of mal-development are dumped on the police like hot potatoes. The location of industries (perceived by people as harbingers of prosperity), linguistic states, communalism, caste-conflicts, reservations of various kinds, SEZs, et al perhaps generated more conflict and violence, than prosperity and happiness, in Indian society. These inadequacies in political management leading to diverse mutations of the Gross Social Conflict have been dumped on the police. The Police leadership had never effectively stated

Table 1: India : Crime at a Glance, 2008

Sl. No.	*Categories Heads*	*Cases reported*	*% to total IPC crimes*	*Rate of Crime*	*Charge-sheeting rate*	*Convic-tion rate*
1	2	3	4	5	6	7
A)	**VIOLENT CRIMES**					
1	MURDER	32766	1.6	2.8	83.2	38.4
2	ATTEMPT TO COMMIT MURDER	28598	1.4	2.5	89.0	31.3
3	C.H. NOT AMOUNTING MURDER	3863	0.2	0.3	87.4	34.8
4	RAPE	21467	1.0	1.9	93.9	26.6
5	KIDNAPPING & ABDUCTION	30261	1.4	2.6	73.4	27.1
6	DACOITY	4530	0.2	0.4	72.0	23.0
7	PREPARATION & ASSEMBLY FOR DACOITY	3217	0.2	0.3	96.7	23.1
8	ROBBERY	20522	1.0	1.8	68.7	30.0
9	RIOTS	66018	3.2	5.7	89.5	20.2
10	ARSON	9249	0.4	0.8	70.0	22.5
11	DOWRY DEATHS	8172	0.4	0.7	92.8	33.4
	TOTAL VIOLENT CRIMES	228663	10.9	19.8	84.2	27.8
B)	**CRIME AGAINST WOMEN (IPC+SLL)**					
1	KIDNAPPING & ABDUCTION OF WOMEN & GIRLS	22939	1.1	2.0	74.1	27.1
2	MOLESTATION	40413	1.9	3.5	96.1	31.7
3	SEXUAL HARASSMENT	12214	0.6	1.1	96.8	50.5
4	CRUELTY BY HUSBAND AND RELATIVES	81344	3.9	7.1	93.7	22.4
5	IMPORTATION OF GIRLS	67	0.0	0.0	72.2	12.3
	TOTAL CRIME AGAINST WOMEN (IPC+SLL)	195856	9.4	17.0	92.5	30.1

1	2	3	4	5	6	7
C)	**ECONOMIC CRIMES**					
1	CRIMINAL BREACH OF TRUST	16487	0.8	1.4	70.6	30.2
2	CHEATING	66579	3.2	5.8	73.7	29.1
3	COUNTERFEITING	2991	0.1	0.3	48.9	38.3
	TOTAL ECONOMIC CRIMES	86057	4.1	7.5	72.1	29.7
D)	**PROPERTY CRIMES**					
1	BURGLARY	93742	4.5	8.1	0.1	0.1
2	THEFT	316761	15.1	27.5	41.5	38.0
	TOTAL PROPERTY CRIMES	410503	19.6	35.6	41.6	38.1
E)	**CRIME AGAINST SC**					
	TOTAL PROPERTY CRIMES	33615	1.6	2.9	90.4	31.7
F)	**CRIME AGAINST ST**					
	TOTAL CRIME AGAINST ST	5582	0.3	0.5	96.0	27.2
G)	**CRIME AGAINST CHILDREN**					
	TOTAL CRIME AGAISNT CHILDREN	22500	1.1	2.0	84.4	35.7
H)	**COGNIZABLE CRIMES UNDER IPC**					
	TOTAL COGNIZABLE CRIMES UNDER IPC	2093379		181.5	79.8	42.6
I)	**COGNIZABLE CRIMES UNDER SLL**					
	TOTAL COGNIZABLE CRIMES UNDER SLL	3844725		333.4	94.6	83.5
J)	**COGNIZABLE CRIMES UNDER IPC+SLL**					
	TOTAL COGNIZABLE CRIMES UNDER IPC+SLL	5938104		515.0	89.5	73.9

Note : A4, A11 ARE PART OF CRIME AGAINST WOMEN ALSO; A6, A7 & A8 ARE PART OF PROPERTY CRIMES ALSO.

Source : Crime in India 2008 Compendium NCRB MHA, GOI, New Delhi 2009 p. 111.

that the police are not the most appropriate institution to manage developmental conflict of that nature and scale. After accepting their expanded role, police organizations have not been prepared to be able to meet the problems of conflict management. The police were being labeled and described as a 'peace force' during the British colonial times. More frequently; the clichéd reference has faded out.

The core issues of national security on one hand, and of the Gross Social Conflict on the other, are competing for primacy of attention. The role of the police as presented in Illustration-9 reveals the dimensions of such an expanding role. In this rapid expansion of load, coupled with competing demands, the cardinal role of the police remains neglected, to say the least. Under such circumstances, the 'system' management spanning a wide range of issues (such as recruitment, induction training, discipline, organizational role-goal clarity, *inter-se* role conflict, morale and motivation of the force, rest and recuperation; coordination, cooperation and intelligence sharing, deployment, performance evaluation, and withdrawal to their respective bases) also gets neglected. Instead, it is a constant

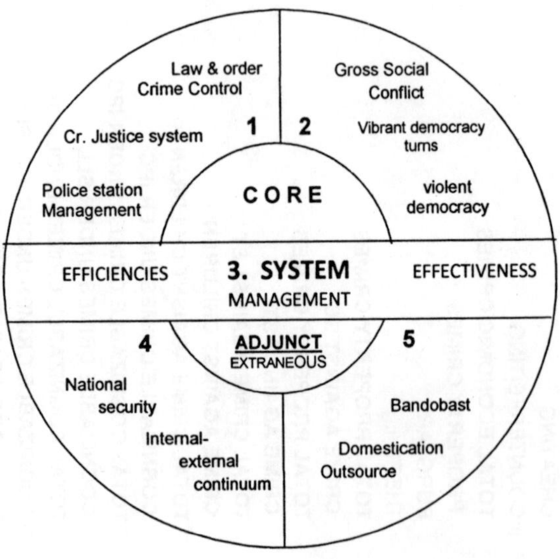

Illustration 9: Expanding Role of Police

fire fighting, even false alarms, in which the police have been at the receiving end.

The cutting-edge of a police organization, its constabulary, are in dire need of training in order not just to make them knowledgeable of human rights, secularism and social conflict, but also to be able to handle such problems as these that arise on the job. At the levels of leadership, facets of commitment to the core values of democracy have to be cultivated so as to internalize such values that reflect their organizational culture. It is the collective, shared set of values that determine and reflect the organizational culture, the cultivation of which is the function of leadership. If any individual develops an interest over and above his team interest, it may be valued as his self-interest, which may grow into a vested interest. The interests of individuals shall never exceed the team interest. That is why it is often held that the best man for a job is not the one with the best of capabilities but one with the greatest commitment.

It is possible to bring about a change in the character of the police and police organizations. Such changes in organizational culture cannot be brought about overnight, through reform merely of the law. Reform and change within the police organizations is a *sine qua non*, for the police to transform themselves, to be able to play the role of socio-legal engineers of the society. Police transformation is a function of police leadership. Indeed such reform is feasible; it could be effective and enduring at the 'local' levels, such as a police station that operates closest to the community. Such initiatives have been found to be very successful. Some recent reports (*The Hindu*, Vizag edition) reveal that officers of the Indian Police Service (Mr. Ravi Krishna, ASP, Chintapalli) have successfully innovated and adopted such approaches while: (a) delivering services at the doorstep of women in distress, (b) meeting people (affected by extremism) individually, (c) addressing the youth attempting suicide out of frustration arising from failure in exams, to think about the agony that his/her mother will undergo, (d) to fight one's cause lawfully rather than killing oneself, and (e) organizing community lunch during communal riots in order to contain passions and sustain harmony. Such guidelines have been incorporated in the Andhra Pradesh Police manual during the year 1998.

Gandhian policing is an ideal mode that can be adopted and acted on at local, community levels, so as to facilitate thinking at the macro, national levels. Police, by the very nature of historical hangovers (as a colonial tool) and statutory responsibilities and duties have acquired a negative image. India, after becoming a democracy, has not attempted seriously to promote a positive image and role-relationship with the people and the community. Some good intentioned initiatives, such as community policing, has emerged still-born due to diverse beliefs and prejudices of both the police and the community; and the still-born has been given a hasty burial even without a *post mortem*.

Police can be the 'educator' on human rights, promoting awareness among the people; insist on remaining above the 'partisan', and shape a proactive role for themselves in promoting social harmony and peace by adapting, adopting and enhancing their own knowledge and skills of conflict resolution at the level of communities. Police have to successfully negotiate with the political, legislative and judicial institutions in their roles as complementary units and that the objectives which emerge from a shared vision and mission are common to all organizations. Gandhian Policing can be a label. It can become a reality only when it is explored, experimented and evaluated, and scaled to a working, operational model. Such a Gandhian model can be triggered of as a professional police initiative. Individual initiatives deserve a serious examination and creative support.

It is observed by Amnesty International, that at least 81 governments the world over practise torture in police custody. Torture can only tarnish police image and efficacy. In the age of terrorism, it is a challenge to the police leadership to fight and contain crime without resorting to torture.

The Police Pantheon

Data presented in Tables 2 and 3 project the fact that the growth of police organizations is keeping, more than keeping up, their ratio with the growth in population. The density of policemen per hundred sq. kms, has also maintained a steady growth although

Table 2: India : Basic Police Data (1996-2006)

Sl. No.	Particulars	1996	1998	2000	2002	2004	2006	% change cover last 11 years
1	Population (1st October – each year) in thousands	939,060	970,932	1,020,631	1,055,051	1,089,915	1,123,993	
			3.34	5.12	3.37	3.30	3.13	19.63
2	Sanctioned strength of Civil Police including Dist. Armed Reserve Police	996,060	1,042,219	1,077,415	1,120,167	1,170722	1,210,742	
			4.63	3.38	3.97	4.51	3.42	21.55
3	Sanctioned strength of State Police Force as on 1.1.2006	350,880	371,383	372,346	348,609	359,667	421,909	
			5.84	0.26	-6.37	3.17	17.31	20.24
4	Sanctioned Strength of Total State Police Force as on 1.1.2006	1,346,940	1,413,602	1,449,761	I,468,776	1,530,389	1,632,651	
			4.95	2.56	1.31	4.19	6.68	21.21
5	Population per Policemen	697.54	686.85	704.00	718.32	712.18	688.45	
			-1.53	2.50	2.03	-0.85	-3.33	-1.30
6	Policemen per lakh (hundred thousand) of Population							
	(i) Civil Police	106.02	107.34	105.56	106.17	107.41	107.72	
			1.25	-1.66	0.58	1.17	0.28	1.61
	(ii) Total Police	143.36	145.59	142.05	139.21	140.41	145.25	
			1.56	-2.44	-1.99	0.86	3.45	1.32
7	Policemen per hundred square kms. Area							
	(i) Civil Police	31.46	32.91	34.03	35.38	36.97	38.24	
			4.63	3.38	3.97	4.51	3.42	21.55
	(ii) Total Police	42.54	44.64	45.79	46.39	48.33	51.56	
			4.95	2.56	1.31	4.19	6.68	21.21

(Contd.)

Sl. No.	Particulars	1996	1998	2000	2002	2004	2006	% change cover last 11 years
8	No. of Police Zones	67	69	64	45	40	43	
			2.99	-7.25	-29.69	-11.11	7.50	-35.82
9	No. of Police Ranges	147	161	157	178	164	166	
			9.52	-2.48	13.38	-7.87	1.22	12.93
10	No. of Police Districts	579	630	635	655	664	673	
			8.81	0.79	3.15	1.37	1.36	16.23
11	Number of Police Sub-divisions	1,440	1,450	1,481	1,514	1,652	1,758	
			0.69	2.14	2.23	9.11	6.42	22.08
12	No. of Police Circles	2,261	2,411	2,452	2,276	2,450	2,456	
			6.63	1.70	-7.18	7.64	0.24	
13	No. of Police Stations	11,838	11,976	12,248	12,445	12,548	12,833	
			1.17	2.27	1.61	0.83	2.27	8.41
14	No. of Police Out-posts	4,897	5,810	6,980	6,943	7,245	7,425	
			18.64	20.14	-0.53	4.35	2.48	51.62
15	Number of State Armed Police Battalions	283	290	307	316	326	365	28.98
		+ 8 Coys	+ 8 Coys	+ 8 Coys	+ 8 Coys	+ 8 Coys	+ 8 Coys	

Total Area of the country is 3,166,4145 Sq. Kms.

Table 3: India : Police in India – Sanctioned Strength of Police in States / UTs

Sl. No.	*States / Union Territories*	*Strength of Civil & Dist. Armed Police*	*Strength of State Armed Police*	*Total Strength of State Police (Civil & Armed)*
(1)	(2)	(3)	(4)	(5)
1	Andhra Pradesh	71,000	17,000	89,000
2	Arunachal Pradesh	3,031	2,689	6,000
3	Assam	16,480	35,813	52,293
4	Bihar	71,321	15,480	86,201
5	Chattisgarh	15,249	10,734	25,983
6	Goa	3,841	631	4,472
7	Gujarat	52,421	12,418	64,839
8	Haryana	47,323	4,702	52,025
9	Himachal Pradesh	8,800	4,948	13,748
10	Jammu & Kashmir	40,958	19,999	60,957
11	Jarkhand	35,535	10,295	45,830
12	Karnataka	73,581	9,886	83,467
13	Kerala	32,617	4,150	36,767
14	Madhya Pradesh	53,074	20,205	73,279
15	Maharashtra	136,129	15,894	152,023
16	Manipur	5,640	9,046	14,686
17	Meghalaya	9,432	3,879	13,311
18	Mizoram	3,130	4,745	7,875
19	Nagaland	8,265	11,687	19,952
20	Orissa	29,341	9,635	38,976
21	Punjab	71,907	18,838	90,745
22	Rajasthan	45,167	25,557	70,724
23	Sikkim	1,808	1,786	3,594
24	Tamil Nadu	82,996	12,688	95,684
25	Tripura	10,584	10,711	21,295
26	Uttar Pradesh	123,272	33,390	156,662
27	Uttaranchal	11,412	3,904	15,316
28	West Bengal	49,799	15,849	65,648
29	A & N Islands	2,183	718	2,901
30	Chandigarh	4,209	419	4,628
31	D & N Haveli	112	88	200
32	Daman & Diu	244	0	244
33	Delhi	46,316	10,887	57,203
34	Lakshadweep	349	0	349
35	Pondicherry	2,406	764	3,170
	All India	1,170,722	359,667	1,530,389

Source: BPR & D (MHA), GoI, New Delhi.
Note: As on 1-1-2008.

there is no normative benchmark for such density. Organizationally, the number of police zones, ranges and districts, number of police sub-divisions, police circles and police stations (including outposts) have maintained a rapid growth. The strength of officers has increased in the country as a whole, as detailed in Table 4.

Table 4: Police in India: Sanctioned Strength of Officers (Civil Police + Armed Police)

Sl. No.	*States / UTs*	*DGP*	*Addl. DGP*	*IGP*	*DIG*	*AIGP/ SSP/SP*	*ASP/ Dy.SP*
(1)	(2)	(3)	(4)	(5)	(6)	(7)	(8)
1.	Andhra Pradesh	5	28	29	42	115	547
2.	Arunachal Pradesh	1	0	1	4	27	59
3.	Assam	4	6	12	19	88	509
4.	Bihar	2	10	19	27	83	383
5.	Chattisgarh	2	5	9	16	53	327
6.	Goa	1	0	0	1	10	27
7.	Gujarat	2	16	24	16	86	237
8.	Haryana	2	5	14	15	76	195
9.	Himachal Pradesh	2	7	13	13	43	125
10.	Jammu & Kashmir	1	4	14	19	162	388
11.	Jharkhand	1	4	11	15	36	252
12.	Karnataka	4	14	28	33	168	390
13.	Kerala	1	8	8	14	65	248
14.	Madhya Pradesh	2	8	20	30	190	653
15.	Maharashtra	[illegible]	13	26	33	218	671
16.	Manipur	1	2	6	9	69	122
17.	Meghalaya	1	4	6	6	36	98
18.	Mizoram	1	0	1	4	23	107
19.	Nagaland	2	2	8	12	35	172
20.	Orissa	2	6	10	17	148	251
21.	Punjab	3	10	17	23	252	525
22.	Rajasthan	2	10	24	26	124	677
23.	Sikkim	1	3	7	8	14	53
24.	Tamil Nadu	7	22	24	38	124	702
25.	Tripura	1	2	6	8	53	211
26.	Uttar Pradesh	9	22	64	71	211	1,118
27.	Uttaranchal	1	2	5	8	17	113
28.	West Bengal	6	20	31	43	104	328
29.	A & N Islands	0	0	1	2	2	13
30.	Chandigarh	0	0	1	0	4	13
31.	D & N Haveli	0	0	0	0	1	1
32.	Daman & Diu	0	0	0	0	1	2
33.	Delhi	1	3	15	6	45	301
34.	Lakshadweep	0	0	0	0	1	1
35.	Pondicherry	0	0	1	0	2	21
	All India	70	236	455	578	2,686	9,840

Source: BPR & D (MHA), GoI, New Delhi.
Note: As on 1-1-2005.

There are various ways of looking at any organization: an overview, an aerial or satellite view, a historical view, an analytical/structural view, or a functional perspective. There is also an internal 'mirror-view – vis-à-vis an outsider's view. Here, a limited historical view is attempted within the context and canvas of a society seeking to turn democratic. The environment, of which police is an integral part, shapes the organization and provides parameters of analysis. These parameters may be tentatively identified thus: (a) growth, (b) role and load expansion de jure, and de facto, (c) structural changes, and (d) transformation in the ethics of police organizations.

The lag between political transition and transformation of the police continues to widen in substantive terms as well as in the time-lag, so much so that the police are out of tune with the demands of a parliamentary constitutional democracy. The several committees, panels and commissions both at the national and state levels on police reform have exposed the dissonance between the (a) political, democratic, constitutional transition and the police organizations – structural and functional, (b) critical variance in the *de jure* and *de facto*, and (c) the urgent need to reform the police aimed at promoting and sustaining their transformation. It is not that the political leadership is not aware of hiatus. But, (collectively) they do not have the will to act and facilitate such a transformation. On their part, the leadership of police organizations give the impression that they feel comfortable to work under a highly 'politicized' ambience – like the proverbial tiger accustomed to the comforts of life in a cage. Accountability for police action (commissions) and inaction (omissions) is owned by the political party/parties in power. Transfers are utilized by the political leaders both as rewards and as punishments; they are so perceived by the police officers.

In our democratic polity, though in its evolving state, even after six decades, the Union Home Minister had to reiterate, post-Mumbai 26/11, that "We do not think anyone can find fault with our determination to fight terror, and the collective political resolve," and that "we will attempt to change the way policing is done", in India.

Table 5: India : Profile of CPOs and PMFs : 2003

Sl. No.	*Central Police Organization*	*Date of foundation*	*Number of*		*Total*	*Number of Batallions as on 2005*
			Gazetted Officers	*Non-gazetted Officers*		
(1)	(2)	(3)	(5)	(6)	(7)	(8)
1	Assam Rifles	1835	850	59,515	60,365	44
2	Central Reserve Police Force	1939	3,796	244,894	248,690	191
3	Indo-Tibetan Border Police	1992	755	35,569	36,324	29
4	Border Security Force	1965	3,744	204,698	208,442	157
5	National Industrial Security Force	1969	1,100	93,165	94,265	279
6	Railway Protection Force		287	68,052	68,339	10
7	Sashastra ** Seema Bal		1,038	30,505	31,543	25
	All India		11,570	736,398	747,968	735
	Coast Guard	1978	1000	—	5200 nos.	6200 nos.
	Rashtriya Rifles	1994	—	—	—	—
	National Disaster Response Force	2010	—	—	—	10
	Intelligence Bureau	1947	20,000	—	—	20,000 nos.
	Central Bureau of Investigation	1963	5,000	—	—	5,000 nos.
	RAW	—	—	—	—	—

Source : BPR&D (MHA)

Notes :

1. Started with 25 Battalions of the State Armed Police Forces.
2. RPF is not a CPO.
3. SSB included non-uniformed component also.

* 271 units + 8 Reserve Battalions.

In the name of police transformation several initiatives have been taken by the various governments, more in the manner of cosmetic experiments, often partisan, and not always in consonance with the reform agenda set out by the various commissions; certainly not in the mode of a holistic overhauling of the way police should be organized, and policing done.

Table 6: Comparison of Country-wise Total Police Personnel and Police-Population Ratio during 2001 and 2002

Sl. No.	*Country*	*Total Police Personnel*			
		Strength of Police		*Strength per 100,000 inhabitants*	
1	2	3	4	5	6
		2001	2002	2001	2002
1.	Italy	320,657	322,483	555.7	559.0
2.	Mexico	448,210	495,821	451.0	491.8
3.	USA	927,759	941,139	325.2	326.4
4.	Australia	57,239	59,812	294.8	304.2
5.	Hungry	28,845	29,113	283.2	286.6
6.	Poland	100,772	99,014	260.8	259.0
7.	United Kingdom	148,932	152,576	252.2	257.6
8.	South Africa	99,520	101,582	222.1	224.0
9.	Switzerland	14,884	14,847	205.8	203.7
10.	Romania	44,670	46,345	199.4	207.8
11.	Nepal	46,444	46,481	196.9	192.7
12.	Chile	29,706	30,090	192.9	193.0
13.	Canada	57,076	58,422	183.6	186.3
14.	Japan	228,000	231,700	179.5	182.2
15.	Myanmar	68,924	68,959	143.1	141.4
		1,428,267	1,433,555	139.1	136.4
16.	India 2003		1,496,276		139.5
	2004		1,530,389		140.4
	2005		1,579,697		142.7
	2006		1,632,651		145.2

Source: UN Division for Policy Analysis and Public Affairs, released on 31 March, 2005 and for India from 2003-2006 'Data on Police Organizations in India', BPR & D.

Post-independence institutional culture of the police and policing have been characterized by a proliferation of structures and a multiplication of tiers, fragmentation of units within organizations, operating in isolation in the manner of 'empires', leading to massive problems of coordination, inadequately supported by appropriate systems, a large volume of under trials, third degree methods, men in uniform (contrary to norms), investigating cases involving women and children, a high degree of centralization, misuse and abuse of powers, statutory as well as discretionary, poor working and living conditions for the police, low performance, political infiltration into the police, and police excesses, and 'lathi'-happy police violence against hapless innocent members of the community. The training imparted does not reflect on the job. The expression 'trigger-happy' cannot be used with reference to the police in India because many of them are placed on the job without having adequate training in arms, and the lathi is their only equipment. Occasionally, in the rush of events, the recruits are asked to bring their uniform at their own expense.

The 'environment' within which the police system operates is changing fast. Police have a mission to fulfil, in translating the dream of "we the people of India", who proclaimed themselves, constituting a democratic republic. People have recognized that relative peace is an essential pre-condition for social transformation to take place. The police system has to perform its role as an instrument of social harmony; in order to be able to do that it has to transform its own organizational culture, in the desirable direction, and at a rapid pace.

There is a wide-range of competing, conflicting and ever expanding demands on the police made by society. Harmonizing these competing and conflicting demands and crystallization of its role is a *sine qua non* before developing organizational capabilities in order to fulfill the assigned mission. Negotiating with the political leadership is a function of police professional leadership.

Vision: Mission: Strategies of the Police in a Democratic Polity

What is a vision? Who and what constitute the reference point for such a vision, and why should any individual, group, institution or a nation have a vision? As people constantly 'interact', within as well as with one another, change is triggered and emerges as the only constant in human society. Such a change is rooted in and revolves around values, interests and identities, crystallized (to different degrees) in terms of ideas, ideals and ideologies; they 'Jell peoples' into a nation. Diversity that may emerge out of pluralism generates a clash of values, interests or identities, leading to varying levels and patterns of social conflict. Conflict may occur, but as it is not inevitable, it can always be resolved. Thus prevention and resolution of conflict also forms a vital, and a constant part of the process of social change.

In the annals of human civilization people on this planet earth have witnessed several factors as well as patterns and levels of conflict – political, armed, economic, social, cultural etc., and methods as well as modes of conflict resolution which is described in the Indian 'tradition' as (The Middle Path), '*Samanvaya*', a synthesis, on the basis of a set of 'higher' order values. As civilizations "advanced", human communities had also developed jurisprudential concepts, methods, and institutions of dispute settlement and conflict resolution. This process can be illustrated with reference to Indian civilization which enunciated and operationalized higher order values and principles such as '*Vasudaika Kutumbakam*' ('the universal family of man'), '*Sarve Janah Sukhino Bhavantu'* (Let all humans, everywhere, be happy), '*Abhyudaya'* (the progression and sustainability of human society) as the end objective of '*Pragati*', measured in terms of material and aggregated economic prosperity, Gross Domestic Product (GDP), per capita income and standard of living. The developmental perspectives can and have been measured in diverse modes on the basis of 'changing' values – such as, when Gandhi had evolved and enunciated that "Man is the measure of development" long before the global society had shifted to measuring development in terms of Human Development Index (HDI). The emergence, 'adoption' of and 'adaptations' in the name of democracy, on a global scale as a desirable norm has illustrated and demonstrated a new wave of 'aspirations' of peoples – both in terms of the concept and modus of 'people-centric' 'inclusive' social (political, economic and cultural) change – a higher order reorganization of social change, through the process of 'socio-legal engineering'.

Every individual, organization and community or society involved in the process of change encounters a diversity of expectations, some measure of discord, competition and conflict seeking harmonization, in tune with certain higher order values, with ideals crystallized within the framework of an ideology. The past, present and future of any society thus constitute a 'continuum', demarcated by the goals and objectives set out by the people at various levels, before the society, global, regional / national/local and harmonized it to different degrees. All the people, all the institutions and all the governments draw from the same ideological springs and fountainheads. But, as different communities are at different stages of development, the phenomena of change emerges in complete configurations. An aggregated process of 'change', at the level of any society, can be mapped out as in Illustration 10.

Change as a Continuum and Constant

→ PAST ⟶	PRESENT ⟶	FUTURE →
→ Factors of change ⟶	Politics & Politicization social Interaction / Churming ⟶	Progression / Evolution
A. Values/Ideologies Liberal democracy – Secularism – Monogamy	**Public Opinion** Expectations Competition / divergence Conflicts	1. Utopia Dream / Vision 2. Millennial Developmental Goals
B. Socio-Economic – Capitalism/ – Socialism – Liberalization	**Political parties** as Prime movers Democratization Consensual / conflict modes	3. Mission: Role: Goal Institutional / Organizational Individual
C. Scientific/ Technological – Immunization – Green Revolution – Tech. Missions	**Public Interest** Harmonization Prioritization Manifesto Mandate	4. Objectives / Goals Institutional–complementarity
D. Global/External – Global warming – Rogue states – US watch on Hu. Rights – WTO/ Free trade	**Social Agenda** Civil Society Participation Competing demands Prioritization	5. Ethical Frame Gandhi's Seven sins "politics without principles" Ends-Means conflict
E. Legitimacy / credibility	**Institutionalization** Constitution of India Liberal democracy Electoral process Manifesto - mandate	6. Commonality of objectives Complementarity of Roles Role/Goal confluence

Illustration 10: Analytical Frame of Macro Level Social Change

Where change is a constant and the ground conditions are constantly in a state of flux, can strategies and actions on security be allowed to remain static and lag behind vis-à-vis societal as well as global situations? The factors of security are changing rapidly. Among the many challenges of change, the threat of nuclear war, sustainability of the global environmental balance, economic debt burden, and terrorism backed by extremism have emerged to the fore, which the nation states are trying to cope with.

The Naxalite leadership holds that killing is a normal phenomenon in any 'movement'. Even in a capitalist society, killings take place. Extremists assert that their policy of annihilation will continue to remain as one of the forms of the Maoist movement".[29] The Prime Minister of India, in one of his references (Nov. 2009) to terrorism indulged in by Naxalite groups, has described it as "the greatest internal threat"[30] to the integrity of the Indian state.

The Leftist movements have proved on the ground, in the Kerala state of India, that they can acquire power as much under (relatively) liberal democratic conditions through the electoral process, as through armed struggle fighting against the democratic government, as in Nepal. In the process, Naxals also may get caught in democratic trappings. The world is moving through an archaic process of change, even under the canopy of liberalization. These 'anarchic' factors and forces are at work carrying diverse labels, causing a multiplex of responses, such as coastal security, Hindu nationalism, social friction on issues such as chanting of *Vande Mataram* in schools. We had envisioned building a secular state but it has become a sick state. We wanted to build up nationalism as a strong bond of internal integration, and as a shield against external terrorist groups operating as a virus, but, anti-democratic forces within are assuming a pandemic character. Issues of global governance as much as the deficit in good governance at the national level, have been identified as at the heart of the ongoing world economic crisis, with a backlash on political and social organizations and processes, everywhere.

Issues of social conflict such as the Babri Masjid incident are getting out of the hands of the political leadership, legislative debates, and beyond the realm of judicial institutions, ending up as 'garbage' to be cleared by police organizations. Political leaders demonstrate their brinkmanship by proposing tribal battalions, minority police, arming the public, and Koya commandos as solutions to social conflict. While the public debate, such propositions, police leadership remains silent on such vital issues of policy. Their thinking is not available to promote public awareness. Choked by the popular and expanding demands on the police for armed guards and plainclothes men to protect MPs, MLAs, PRI functionaries, religious institutions, et al it was almost for the first time, that a woman police officer remarked.[31] "It is humanly impossible to provide security to all categories". Whole communities, such as tribals, are antagonized and reduced to becoming hostile towards the administration in general and the police in particular. People from the tribal communities are sandwiched between the police and the extremists. Public administrators and members of tribal communities consider and address each other as the 'sons-in-law' of the government.

The Indian police may proudly claim the adoption and adaptation of "rubber bullets" innovated by the Czech Police in their effort to reduce citizen fatalities in instances of confrontation and disorder emerging from social conflicts. But, chocked by the demands for intervention in situations created by politically instigated or supported mob-violence, police has no option but to resort to excessive force and weapons of firing, leading to fatalities. Every such situation ends up with demands for inquiry into police action, not the cause of conflict. It is a common place observation that police use excessive force and marshal evidence to secure convictions. The paradox is that under democratic norms and human rights conventions, the Indian police, as the protectors of human rights and promoters of rule of law become the worst violators of human rights, and thus destroyers of the rule of law. It is under these conditions, choking the Indian police organizations, that the several global and international organizations operate as the Global Police, monitoring human rights, religious freedom vis-à-vis suppression of religious and ethnic 'minorities'.

The US Commission on International Religious Freedom (USCIRF) had recommended designating India as a "country of particular concern" in regard to rights of minorities , focusing on

Indian Christians. While the Indian Government had rejected a proposal by the USCIRF to visit and to discuss with officials on conditions of religious freedom with the religious minorities, a group of diplomats from the western hemisphere had visited the state of Orissa to interact with the Christian victims.

All the state police forces have been expanding in battalions and all the CPOs and PMFs have been set up in response to the constantly growing, diverse demands of national integrity and security. Has the overall growth been planned in regard to prevailing levels of conflict and threat perceptions? and a clear appreciation of the role of police, if any, as a peace force? What has been the role of specialized organizations entrusted with research, organizational development, training, monitoring and evaluation of the police organizational units, and their operations? Finally, has there been any internal 'think-tank' organization/process within the police, and if so, what has been their response and contribution to the constant demands of 'redesign' and 'development' of the diverse police organizations?

In view of the organizational proliferation and rapid expansion, what is the nature and level of role clarity and *inter se* role relationships, efficacy of joint operations among the vast network of police organizations? What are the design parameters for the complementary tasks? Many more facets of hierarchy, command and control and 'status' orientations had emerged to the fore, repeatedly in the police organizations and operations. How are political decisions at the national and/or state levels converted into operational norms and goals to the CPOs, PMFs, and the state police forces in the joint management of operations such as for eg. left wing extremism? Such operational norms, perhaps, will also help clarify the role-relationship as between the judicial and police organizations for, the police personnel and organizations often end up with strictures from the judiciary, •*post facto*. Such operational norms will also help promote complementarity between the police and judicial organizations with shared responsibilities and common organizational objectives.

Police are expected to contain and eliminate any threat to the integrity of the democratic character of the nation. How far can they remain committed and uphold the 'democratic ethic' while fighting anti-democratic forces on one front, and the advocates of civil liberties, and human rights on the other. Can the police leadership take umbrage under the lax societal standards to explain away that "police is a part of the society and hence the police can't be faulted if they reflect the sliding standards of the society"? What are the safeguards, normative and institutional, to protect the police who perform challenging and conflicting roles in situations of institutional overlaps and social conflicts?

Issues of synergy emerge in the co-optation and joint operations among the state, the central police organizations, and the armed forces in diverse combinations in respect of deployment, command and control, training and development for such operations in different situations. Cooption boosts synergy, but, hierarchy (real or perceived), negates and kills the productive performance of organizations.

Civil defence and home guards are 'dedicated' to the service of the community, render valuable support to the local administration and to the police in the maintenance of law and order, maintenance of essential services, control and regulation of traffic, and help in the management of various important events such as elections, and fairs and festivals. These organizations are also expected to play an important role in the management of disasters – disaster mitigation and preparedness creating awareness among masses and building capacities of communities to be able to face, mitigate and also avert potential disasters. With the proliferation of police organizations, sub-units, and levels across the length and breadth of the country intra as well as inter-organizational interface management has assumed criticality.

While it would be interesting to undertake a full-fledged and exhaustive analysis of these issues especially from the standpoint of the police, a select set of issues illustrate the ideal modes and extant realities of interface management. India is perhaps the only federal polity with federal crimes but without a federal policy and statutory provisions, until 2010, to deal with crimes across the boundaries of states, and an agency to deal with such crimes. When the national debate gets so skewed, what happens is exactly what we had witnessed. It took a terrorist attack (Mumbai, November

2008) for the nation to have a stringent statute and a federal agency, as the National Investigation Agency (NIA). The Mumbai terrorist attack (November 2008) also shocked the nation on the status of the naked, unguarded coastline that warranted a strong maritime force with adequate reach, endurance and capability.

Though the nation was steeped in terrorist attacks, across the nation anywhere and anytime of their choice, the political dispositions have not helped the enactment of a stringent Federal Police Act. The deployment of central police, para-military forces, and the army is demanded by almost all the states whenever the states felt vulnerable. Most significantly, all the political parties involved in running the governments had conceded that the state civil police were highly subject to partisan politics and hence lost, to a significant level, both efficacy and image in the eyes of the public at large. For all the challenging tasks of policing, the states unabashedly depend upon the deployment of the central police forces. Yet the states run by different regional political parties have been vociferous about the autonomy of the states.

In the Indian context where human rights jurisdiction encompasses political, economic, social and cultural dimensions in an interwoven pattern, the several 'Rights' organizations, like the National and the State Human Rights Commissions, the Women's, the Children's, the Tribals, the Minorities', the S.C. B.C. Commissions, and a plethora of ad hoc Commissions and Committees, along with the political parties, assumed that it is the police who are responsible for the promotion and protection of the entire basket of human rights, holding them responsible for deficiencies. By their inadequate response to this situation, the police admitted, unwittingly though, an image of 'deficiency' in their own performance. This hapless projection of the police, could be dangerous and counter-productive in the long run, not merely to the police but more so to the democratic polity and to the rule of law in the aggregate. The absence of a State Security Commission, as a buffer, as a protective shield, as a regulatory mechanism, to ensure adoption and internalization of certain performance standards makes police forces vulnerable.

Police have three sets of professional codes of ethical conduct. It doesn't require much of research to state that the police are not in a position to comply with any provisions of the three codes of conduct. Viewed one way, if an organization fails, to any degree, the leadership should take the blame. The leadership factor emerged as a critical variable in crippling the police force in the Mumbai attack (of Nov. 2008). The Committee of Ram Pradhan (a former civil servant) and V. Balachandran (a retired Intelligence Officer) had observed, *inter alia*, (1) "no formal debriefing sessions were held with all groups of officers to make an assessment of what went wrong; (2) gross violations of standard operating procedures; (3) for the most part, though, the leaderless force was left to cope with the situation as best as it could; (4) bad leadership also led to the mishandling of the one force which could have facilitated a sharper police response; and (5) the Quick Response Teams were dispersed over multiple locations, depending on the demands of local commanders, a violation of a cardinal tenet of special forces operations. In retrospect, it can be stated that such things happen over a long period of time.

In the wake of terrorism and extremism, inadequacies of Intelligence apparatus has been projected in different ways in different countries. In the USA, the 9/11 Commission appointed by the U.S. Congress is expected to severely indict the CIA for its failure to predict the 2001 Al-Qaeda attack on the U.S. The then Director of the CIA, (George Tenet) had put in his papers, in anticipation and possibly to prompt such an eventuality.

In the U.K. the dominant feeling was that MI6 did not correctly advise the Prime Minister, (Tony Blair) on the presence of (weapons of mass destruction) in Iraq. There is a continual debate on how to make the intelligence community more responsive and responsible to the country's needs in a dynamic world.

In India, the Congress Party, had pledged in one of its major policy documents that it would remove some palpable shortcomings in the country's national security infrastructure.

It is in this background, of inadequacies in the intelligence operations, a former senior Intelligence Bureau (IB) official in his publication[32] outlines India's vision and the challenges that lie ahead in achieving that vision. Drawing from a host of sources, he believes that we have to strive hard to take our rightful place in the comity of nations, taking advantage of our core strengths in areas such as satellite technology, IT services, automobile ancillaries, pharmaceuticals and telecommunication. If India has to march forward without any disruption, we need a stable social situation, complemented by peace in the neighbourhood. It is this perspective that demands organization of our intelligence collection and analysis on modern professional lines. Nath's scan of the problems haunting continually covers the troubled Jammu & Kashmir situation and the contribution thereto by the infamous ISI of Pakistan, the violence perpetrated by a wide spectrum of militant groups in the Northeast, the obsolete casteist passions that retard progress in some parts of the country and the most serious of all our ills, the unabated corruption in public life that has shamefully remained unchecked.

The question is how fast and adequate is the quality of cooptation, in sharing intelligence and acting together by the institutions who have been operating within a hierarchial ambience? Indian intelligence organizations and thus the police organizations have not quickly, nay rapidly, come together to establish synergic interaction and action. This goes to the advantage of forces inimical to the nation. Inactions and unsynchronized actions reveal that the heavy flow of intelligence, from many quarters is not smooth. Credit goes to the terrorist groups and their 'thunder-bolt' attacks for the urge to streamline security organizations in India.

The multiplex of issues such as: (a) creation of new organizations, or units (like Rapid Action Force within the CRPF where the midwife forgot to cut-off the umbilical cord), or new levels without a clear role-delineation, diffused inter-face management, (b) policy proclivity to create 'new' organizations rather than redesign, reengineer and reform the existing organizations, (c) reducing reform to tinkering of structures without matching management systems, leading to confusion and frustration in deployment, command and control, (d) fanciful, ill-conceived notions such as tribal police (in the specific context of Naxalism), minority police (in the context of communal conflict),

Salwa Judum in the state of Chhattisgarh – which aggravated turbulence, (e) increasing, overnight, battalions of police, as a means to solve the problem of unemployment; (f) weaving together contradictory strands of 'reform' such as proliferation of levels, (15 DGs and 15 ADGPs within a state) and hierarchies in terms of zones, ranges, divisions et al, and installing IT based communication cutting decision-making levels leading to a high degree of centralization, with the attendant consequences: (i) mismatch between autonomy, responsibility and accountability on the one hand, (ii) authoritarianism emerging from depriving (especially at the middle tiers of leadership), a sense of participation in decision-making, and in the end, demotivation, and frustration). The demoralization may be for two different sets of reasons such as dilution of role at the level of leadership as reflected by one senior IPS officer who observed that "we are professionals but working for an unprofessional organization", and at the cutting edge level of constabulary due to lack of protection (from the onslaught of political leadership and powerful lobbies) in the performance of their role with the consequence of a sense of 'withdrawal' from duties and responsibilities, and frustration writ large among the constabulary forcing them to be trigger happy and corrupt (making hay while the sun shines). There is an absence of any internal/external mechanism and process, of criteria-based evaluation of accountability and performance of police organizations.

These internal inadequacies expose the police organizations to negative perceptions and adverse stereotypes of the police organizations as a whole. The young leadership characterized by ideals of serving the society and as opting for the Indian Police Service (IPS) as a profession, and the honest and efficient senior officers as well nurturing a feeling of mistaken choice for the IPS, leaves an adverse impact on their job satisfaction, leading to a sense of 'withdrawal'.

The constitutional scheme of "commonality of objectives" and "complementarity of roles" as between the legislative, executive and judicial institutions may get distorted when any one of these seem to 'correct' the deficiencies or distortions of any other subsystem. When such inter-institutional role conflict emerges to the fore, citizens tend to perceive such conflicts as (a) arising from constitutional language and interpretation, or as (b) these institutions are over-playing their role as a part of the unstated power-play. Such a role-conflict is evident in the case of Gujarat where the Supreme Court set up a Special Investigation Team (SIT), headed by a retired director of the CBI. The Government of Gujarat set up a judicial Commission of Inquiry, while the Ministry of Railways set up yet another committee headed by a retired judge of the Supreme Court, who beats all others, delivering its report to the Ministry of Railways, which releases the report within hours. While the inter-institutional trauma is inflicted on the public, an in-service senior police officer of the Gujarat cadre 'discloses' during May 2011, full ten years after the event, that he was subjected to pressure by the Chief Minister of Gujarat. The disclosure of an in service police officer amounts to a confession, even if abetted by a political executive. Such festering wounds on the body politic not only dilute the legitimacy and credibility of the system as a whole, but also provide fresh feed-stock to the political power-house. The involvement of the National Human Rights Commission (NHRC) in the Gujarat episode did not create any ripples, as the NHRC had already lost its credibility in the eyes of the public. It is high time that the Indian State sets right the *inter se* relations between the police and the judiciary, as a *sine qua non*, for the police performance to improve.

The police as a profession has a professional role in the formulation of policies concerning internal security management, peace keeping, and protection and promotion of the all pervasive human rights in Indian democracy. What is the reality on the ground? Some may debate both within and outside the police organizations whether policing constitutes a profession. While the policy is formulated by the polity, and legitimized by the political, democratic, legislative processes, police do have a role in shaping the policy, but the police have to translate the policy into action on the ground. But in India, if the political process has edged out the police from the policy process, the police have come to accept the situation by default.

Evaluation of the police, their role and performance emerges as the most critical variable from the standpoint of Article 356 of the Constitution of India – which provides for the Union to take over the administration of a state in case law and order has failed. Police is responsible for law and order. What are the professional inputs of the police to the Union while considering dismissal of a state government and to impose President's Rule? It is in this context that (a) the constitutional rationale for and character of an all-India police service, and (b) the need for a State Security Commission (as a buffer between the police and the political process and) as a regulatory mechanism emerge. This foundational parameter is totally negated by all the political parties in Indian democracy, as demonstrated in the form and manner of the mass-transfers of IPS officers, as the first official action by every Chief Minister, literally, soon after he/she is sworn into office. Any modicum of isolated resistance proves an exception to the law. Consequently, extra legal and illegal political directives operate as the prime mover of police in India. This is the scenario of police organizations, their role, and their performance that shapes the external interface of police management. The external 'interface' encompasses the Judiciary (with its autonomous status and stature and a fairly well defined role), the civil administration, the armed forces, the media, the newly emerging third-tier of decentralized Panchayati Raj Institutions, the civil society institutions at different levels within the nation (NGOs, the PUCL, and the Amnesty International at the international level). This interface is even more challenging especially as the police are directly 'controlled' by the political institutions – different political parties in varying (and constantly shifting) political 'alliance and alliance *Dharma*'.

Institutional interface management has to be crafted carefully, with a mutually respected network of reciprocal relationships, shared values, shared vision, common objectives and complementary roles , beyond mere, formal 'cooperation'. They need to co-optate and thus gel, with a clear understanding of command and control in any joint operation and management. Such cooptation is vital in order to ensure synergy and effectiveness.

Left Wing Extremism is held out by the Prime Minister, repeatedly, as the number one internal security problem of the nation. The Ministries of Home and of Defence of the Government of India have been actively engaged in the formulation and shaping of the proposed involvement of the army and the air force. It was in this context, that the army and the air force are hesitant to take on a greater role on the ground, envisaging that such involvement could result in collateral damage. There appears to be a view emerging that the army should step in only as a last resort in tackling the internal law and order situation. It was also opined that the presence of soldiers in civilian areas could lead to a sense of alienation among the local population. As the Maoists seem to have gained the sympathy of and rapport with the 'local', 'tribal' populations, involvement of armed forces could lead to further alienation among the tribal communities where the basic necessities of life and amenities are acutely lacking, even 60 years after the constitutional promise. Understandably, the Defence Ministry holds the view that the task of taking on naxalite issues belongs to the state police.

How is it that in the face of such a wide ranging public discourse on the diverse issues of internal security, the public is deprived of an opportunity and benefit of the opinion of the police, and the various 'think-tank' organizations like the Bureau of Police Research and Development (BPR & D), or the Sardar Vallabhbhai Patel National Police Academy (SVPNPA), or from professional associations such as the Police Science Congress? What is the role, if any, of police as a peaceforce? These are some of the dynamics of inter-face management; by no means exhaustive. What are the dispositions of state police organizations and their leadership, and the Bureau of Police Training and Research to the idea of Army training the civil police that might generate adverse / superior-subordinate dispositions, especially, when there is such an extensive network of police training academies, colleges and schools spread all over the country? No doubt there are joint programmes of training that are needed to manage joint operations whether short-term, medium-term or long-term; and such programmes are designed and organized, e.g. as between the police, the CRPF as well as the armed forces, to meet the challenges of natural calamities and disaster management, mass emergencies, nuclear and chemical emergencies in civilian areas, floods and natural calamities.

In the case of the judiciary – police inter-face, the judiciary as an autonomous, constitutional entity, stands out at a domineering position compared to the police who do not have a status of autonomy, much less parity. The police fight anti-democratic forces, within the framework of democratic norms. Their efficacy is measured in terms of convictions obtained – where they suffer problems of the criminal justice law and system in regard to 'lack of evidence', inadmissibility of police witneses, non-cooperation from the citizens, and also in regard to 'jail-bail' dilemma and other dichotomies of the system. The visible symbol of the majesty of law, the constable, 'stands' as a hapless employee, before the courts of law. After all, the police is only one of the institutional actors in the promotion, protection and sustenance of rule of law. But, all the deficiencies emerging from multiple players in this regard are not only not appreciated; but police become an easy prey in the blame-game.

Amnesty International (AI) in its annual report of 2010 has observed that both the police and the Maoists violated human rights in Chhattisgarh and in the adjoining states in India during 2009. AI also maintained that the Government failed to ensure accountability for the earlier cases of human rights abuses.

The Peoples Union for Civil Liberties (PUCL) stated that around 40,000 people belonging to tribal communities were displaced due to the conflict between police and Maoists in different states. Of them about 20,000 were living in camps and the remaining took shelter in the neighbouring states.

PUCL had also maintained that authorities had harassed human rights defenders for exposing violations. The arena of human rights conflict was not just confined to the rights organizations of the civil society like the PUCL, but expanded to include the media, as illustrated in the incident where Anil Majumdar was shot dead allegedly by the Assam Police, while trying to mediate peace between the state officials and the banned United Liberation Front of Assam (ULFA). As a peace force, police leadership suffers from fear of both success and failure.

While domestic conflict and violence as an element of internal security is considered as an internal matter of governance and sovereignty, and thus out of bounds of other sovereign states, the United States though itself a sovereign state, considers appropriate to project human rights issues in other sovereign states, as a matter of concern. The Canadian High Commission's (Government's) action in denying visa to a retired Border Security Force Head Constable on grounds that the "BSF is a notoriously violent paramilitary unit" which is "responsible for war crimes in India" proved to be an even more serious instance of sovereign nations, acting in a flagrant and provocative manner on issues of internal security matters and security forces. Do the Indian Police have adequate and appropriate policy frameworks to deal with such situations? Based on available data in regard to the Bhopal gas tragedy, or on the premise of reciprocity, the Indian Police do not seek and secure such policy support in discharging their responsibilities.

The Supreme Courts (May 2010), ruling on narco-analysis, brain-mapping and polygraph tests on the accused, suspects or witnesses, as unconstitutional and a violation of their right to privacy, has been seen by the police organizations as a setback to scientific investigation. Maintaining that the CBI has always taken the consent of the accused before conducting narco-analysis, brain-mapping and polygraph tests, and court permission, the CBI has stated that the Supreme Court ruling is a setback as well as a challenge to forensic science and scientific investigation. How and how far will the ruling would impact on the scientific investigation of crime, and the percentage of convictions, in the face of increasing crime and its technological sophistication? The challenges and contradictions before the police in India today are many; silence cannot be a response, for it suggests acceptance of the status quo.

The debate over phone intercepts by the police has revolved around its possible misuse and abuse at the political level; and the consequent idea of a total ban on intercepts had assumed the popular pattern, as if it is a matter between, the 'ruling' and the 'opposition' political parties. The debate had not focused on the right to privacy, fighting the anti-democratic and anti-national forces by the police, or a consideration of issues of public interest, redefinition of the problem, policy options and implications of alternative, and above all of choices for future action. In the disastrous case of derailment of the Howrah-Kurla (Jnaneswari) Express train, the CID of the Paschim Medinipur district of West Bengal had claimed that it was intercepts of telephonic conversations of several rebel leaders that gave them (the police) 'definite evidence'.

In the complex process of democratic constitutional governance, the various instrumentalities of state, and institutions of civil society perform different tasks in a complementary manner in order to fulfill common objectives as assigned by the constitution. Since a pluralist polity with the heavy drag of historical (socio-economic and cultural) factors generate competing and often conflicting demands on these instrumentalities and institutions, an important role of the institutional leadership is to harmonize and prioritize these competing and conflicting societal demands into their respective organizational missions and objectives within the framework of the vision of the society.

In the Indian context, the internal security scenario and its management is becoming a challenge due to the inadequate processing of the 'conflicting' demands. The dominant ethos of organizations in India is to operate in relative isolation and exclusivity. The crystallization of their respective missions and attunement of 'objectives', constitute the function of organizational leadership which is almost conspicuous by its absence in the police. Policy (with all its inadequacies and distortions) is taken as 'given', whereas under ideal conditions, the policy span of the executive encompasses, inter-alia, 'the shaping of policy'.

Issues of interface between the legislative and the executive, the executive and the judiciary, the police and the para-military forces (PMFs) the civilian and the armed forces, the police and the media, and other institutions of civil society surface with consistent regularity in India. They are sought to be reconciled, at best, in an *ad hoc* rather than in an enduring systemic manner.

This is illustrated in the observation of the Supreme Court: "Ordinarily, a court should refrain from interfering at a premature stage of the inquiry (of a crime) as that may derail and demoralize the investigation", the Supreme Court has cautioned: "Of late, the tendency to interfere in the investigation is on the increase and courts should be vary of possible consequences." Hopefully such an observation from the highest court would have a positive impact.

It may be a war of words, between the South Block and the North Block of the seat of power in New Delhi regarding repeated weapon losses in the north-east. Perceptions of the Election Commission about the scale of deployment as its exclusive prerogative; the army top brass publicly stating that the army is not receiving the required support from the administration, from the Judiciary and other law-enforcing agencies in the North East. All these and many more of the problems of interface have an adverse effect on the system of governance as a whole. Lack of attunement between the CPOs and the state police in extremist infested areas has led to inter-institutional crisis and conflict, and occasional instances of the state police turning informants to the extremists about the movement of men of CPOs and PMFs. The policy as obtaining on paper proclaims that the CPOs and PMFs would aid and assist the state police. But, at the ground level the perceptions reflect that the CPOs/PMFs step in wherever the state police has either proved inadequate or has failed. Such a dissonance between the various institutions would prove an ideal situation for insurgents as well as alien organizations to fish in troubled waters.

Intelligence is a major factor that negates institutional synergy and contributes to discord and neutralization of security institutions. It is to cap this type of problems that a number of attempts have been made to promote pooling and sharing of intelligence. A report of the Standing Committee has stated that "the Committee has been informed that while there is no proposal to increase the numerical strength of the Central Intelligence Bureau, effective steps are being undertaken to reorganize it and increase the ratio of officers so as to improve the quality of human resource manning it." Maintaining that some State intelligence agencies lacked 'professionalism', the Standing Committee held that central intelligence could not be effective without the cooperation of State counterparts. "Knowledge of local conditions, familiarity with topography, local contact at the grass-root level, knowledge of suspected criminal elements right down to the village level and constant vigilance of subversive activities are the essential requirements of proper intelligence and they cannot be ensured by the Intelligence Bureau alone. In this context, it has been brought to the notice of the Committee that some of the state intelligence agencies are lacking in professionalism."

Until the terrorist attack of 26/11 in Mumbai, Andhra Pradesh state alone had a professionally trained counter insurgency force in the form of Grey Hounds. Following the Mumbai attack and a directive from the Union Government, commando forces have been formed from out of the existing manpower, in all the states excepting Kerala. Kerala had initiated the process of a special recruitment through written test, physical efficiency test and specialized training for 200 personnel, in small groups of 30 to 40 members of a composite nature. These small groups would have specialists in super attacks, assaults, para-diving, underwater operations, communication, vehicle interception and planning. These groups would be placed in different parts of the state, each with a base station with facilities for continual training. Apart from the most modern weapons, (not the vintage World War II rifles) the force members may be imparted *Krav Maga*, the hand-to-hand combat evolved by the Israeli army, which has proved effective in counter terrorist strikes.

Reform, redesign and reengineering of the police pantheon is admittedly a crying need, yet not much happens because of hesitation on the part of political leaders and parties. Presently, reform is reduced to organizational proliferation and structural tinkering. Police reform is being delayed at the cost of democracy and all that it stands for.

Hostile Community: Frustrated Police

The patterns of relationships between the police personnel and police organizations on the one hand, and members of the public on the other are dynamic, changing on the basis of situations, nature of perceptions, mutual expectations, relative experiences, either positive or negative dispositions. They shape somewhat enduring mutual attitudes. These relationships and attitudes throw up several dichotomies that coexist as parallel realities, but not as universal or frozen, static images.

There are several studies of public perceptions that projected the police in India as very hard working, sustaining, promoting, and abiding by the cardinal characteristic of 'rule of law'; sustaining a democratic social order, dedicated to duty, with respect for the citizens and human rights, characterized by high integrity and efficacy. At the organizational level, in the aggregate, Malabar Police was held in a high level of esteem. There is, on the other extreme of the spectrum, public opinion, that the police are the most corrupt, partisan, in-disciplined, inefficient, lawless, oppressive, brutal, arrogant, communal, and casteist, having a nexus with the criminal gangs *et al.* It was no less than a judge of the Allahabad High Court, Justice A.N. Mulla, speaking from the Bench, in India's first decade of democracy, who had observed that the police in India represent the most lawless, organized force, the most corrupt and criminal group, in uniform. Justice Mulla had voiced the opinion of a broad spectrum of the Indian society. If that was the scenario in the 1950s, the subsequent decades have not witnessed any significant, positive changes.

Viewed from a different perspective the self-esteem of the constabulary in India is more adverse and negative than the public image of police personnel and of the organizations. Among the officers, the self-perception is reflected that the individuals are 'professionals', but the police organizations are 'unprofessional', reducing the individual functionaries to a state of non-professionals.

The police-public relationships can be seen from yet another dynamic angle, at the level of variations between the states. The 'Malabar Police' evoked, until during the early decades of India's Independence, an image of 'terror' among the public – in preventing and controlling mass behaviour. The mere word that the Malabar Police is being deployed in a crowd situation would contain the crowd behaviour, half the job got done without using the baton, a water cannon, a rubber bullet, or even one round of firing in the air. It was the 'image' of efficacy, of a disciplined force, that used to do the job. The contemporary public 'image' of the police is characterized and shaped by police 'atrocities' as a 'lathi-force', in human behaviour with female members in any group/crowd situation, assault on citizens of the fair sex who visit the police stations to register a grievance or an atrocity, extensive range of corruption, non-registration of complaints, booking, or threats to thrust false implication and use of third-degree methods.

There have been many instances of senior police officers stating that "after all, police are also part of the society and hence reflect all the degraded and declining standards and aberrations obtaining in the society, such officers ignore the fact that the police as an organized, uniformed force that cannot merely reflect, but have to arrest trends of lawlessness in the society. That the police, in fact is the only organization having not one or two, but as many as three codes of conduct – formulated by the United Nations (1979), the MHA Government of India (1985), and the Police themselves (1960). Not many in the police organizations know of the existence of three codes of conduct and behaviour, let alone compliance with them.

It is in this scenario, the absence of a periodic assessment of changing 'images' of police and public expectations that provide the benchmark of images, dispositions and attitudes. The fluctuations in the images of the various state police organizations also reveal as well as shape the mutual dispositions of police and the public. Maharashtra and Tamil Nadu, almost stood at the top of positive images of police on the multiple criteria of efficacy and effectiveness. It is difficult to say, even on the basis of popular images as to which state stood next to Maharashtra and Tamil Nadu. It keeps fluctuating. Whether there is any competition to attain the position of excellence among the state police organizations, formally or informally, is not traceable. The police-public relationships, patterns, and changes are not just reciprocal, but differential and dynamic on the basis of situational factors, and performance standards.

The political parties as the prime movers of India's constitutional democratic transformation have themselves shifted their focus from that of managers of social transformation, to that of seekers of power *per se* as the end objective. They have cultivated corruption of police to the state of an enduring culture of police organizations. Police organizations have emerged as the most effective instruments of partisan power. People at large are clearly aware of this slide, as an extant reality.

Police, described appropriately as the 'peace force' at the advent of democracy, could not erase their erstwhile image as an alien force of the yester decades, serving the sole purpose of the imperial powers, transformed itself into a force that is serving the political bosses protecting their partisan interests. It was easy to continue old habits, so different from the challenges of transforming itself into a democratic force, as a peace force, dedicated to the socio-legal engineering of the Indian society. It was not impossible to transform the role and character of the police. That's why, the Home Minister of India had observed in 2010, full sixty years later, "We have to change the way' policing is done in India."

The situation is made complex and challenging with the 'radical' change in the social setting, the globalization (of democratic ethic), liberalization of economies, revival of 'crusade' and *Jihad* scenarios, religious fundamentalism, induced conversions, extremism, terrorism et al. It is as a part of this globalization with a renewed accent on material culture, and loss of the credibility of institutional network both at the global and national levels of governance. The institutions, are not only atrophied but have acquired 'adversarial' culture with people. India's democracy has turned turbulent and violent in less than half a century; with full potential as a 'regressive' democracy, a 'numerical' democracy and a 'violent' democracy. From the standpoint of the citizens, India cannot be reduced to a placebo-democracy.

That Indian democracy is in a state of disarray is demonstrated by the fact that the public discourse on social conflict and security dominates the media in an all-pervasive manner. It can be illustrated in order to indicate the setting in which the police and public are equally confused as to the situation they are trapped in. As the nation slides into the vortex of communal, caste, regional, human rights, ethnic, extremist and an all-conceivable and all pervasive conflict, the institutions, including especially the police, are caught in the matrix of role conflict. If such conflict had been initially confined, in the centre-state-local frame on the vertical levels, and the legislative-judicial-executive units on the horizontal level, the multifarious human rights organizations, pounce upon the police, seek parallel probes, and condemn the police in the aggregate. The Godhra train carnage case is a classic example. The original tragedy of more than 200 lives lost has been lost sight of in the fight over jurisdictions. The false calls of religion and of disputes about religious symbols in an expanded and multiple historical time frame on the one hand, and the contemporary overnight emergence of religious structures and flash clashes over their regulation, operate today, like cordless, remote-controlled, unmanned machines guided by 'communal flares'. How can the police help themselves as a neutral force dedicated to harmony and development.

As the political parties 'Ruling', 'Opposition' as well as the eternal 'fence sitters' – all of them, plunge into the arena of communal passions with their partisan dispositions, the Supreme Court had to call for clarity of policy in regard to unauthorized religious structures. In the Indian variant of democracy, whistle blowers watch and publicize wrongdoing, such 'public cooperation' leads them to a hell on earth, while wrongdoers go scot free – so frequently that the Prime Minister had to take the initiative in the framing of a legislation on Public Interest Disclosure and Protection of Informants Bill, 2009.

When the head of a police force expresses his 'professional' view on some critical public issue, politicians who arrogate to themselves, the right to confuse the public, condemn such expression of professional views, and also publicly go the extra mile seeking 'an apology' from the head of police for the act of publicly expressing professional views. Prejudices and fears not only prevail in the society, but they determine the quality of democracy and quality of policing.

When the Union Home Ministry ambitiously prepared and proposed to set up a National Intelligence Grid (Natgrid) by pooling intelligence inputs from the various law enforcement and intelligence agencies, the cabinet sub-committee on security had withheld the same on grounds of safeguards and potential misuse of such information, strangely, for political ends, just as the same old debate over POTA, had not focused on the need, but fear of and potential political, partisan misuse and abuse of law.

When proposals are not scrutinized keeping also in view the public perceptions, they boomerang. Quota for minorities stands as one such glaring example. Perceptions get frozen as enduring attitudes. A police constable on traffic duty, was dragged on the road, by a moving vehicle after jumping the red light. Two motor cycle borne drunken citizens shot at a constable when he tried to stop them. A lady went to a police station to register a complaint, and was molested by a constable on duty. In all these and in many other similar instances, the incidents have led to flash politicization of the partisan type, and on one occasion to communal clashes between the Hindus and Muslims, just because one of the violators of the law was a Muslim and the victim happened to be a Hindu. The first reaction of the police in cases of a woman complainant about abuse at the station, is total denial of wrongdoing, but when the agitated public raise the tempo and duration of protest, the police leadership exhibit an added sense of over-protectiveness, may be for 'fear of loss of image' of the police. That is what precisely happens, at the political level where under police and political pressure, the Home Minister first defends the police, but when the 'opposition' parties join the chorus, a probe is conceded, and the concerned functionary is suspended or transferred. Distortions creep into the public perceptions and dispositions become hostile. In the event of an unfortunate Jail break, the opposition invariably hurls charges of police-collusion; the intention being to hurt the 'ruling party'. In the process, the image of the police is tarnished, the public perception of the police and thus public-police relations and mutual attitudes get distorted. The Police and their leadership must recognize that 'political' protection can only damage their own image – the police personnel and their own organization.

Police in India are 'trapped' in an ever-expanding role, load and jurisdiction, they suffer from fatigue factor, because of continuous deployment. In the case of the CRPF, the fatigue factor is acute. The CRPF is no more a 'reserve' force, if anything, it is the most over-used force. The nature of problem situations they are deployed is the most variegated. The fatigue factor has been found, repeatedly, to serious consequences to the police forces, in respect of image, discipline and performance. The BSF, when deployed in interior naxalite areas, had faced, rather frequently, allegations and inquiries of torture of civilians/ villagers 'forcing' them into confessing that they were Maoists. Police undermine their own credibility in the society when they implicate, knowingly, innocent people and present untenable cases in the courts of law. They may be caught in the incessant political discourse and cross-fire on fundamentalism, terrorism and extremism. The recurring public accusations by the Muslim leadership that members of their community are being charged of extremist violence; coupled with demands for maintaining a 'balance' between communities has to be reconciled in a manner as to maintain the 'image' of the police. "Hindu Right' is a new political idiom that has emerged as a political response to the 'communalization' of crime; it has accentuated the hiatus in the form of communal divide, and has sucked the police into stereotypes. In such an ambience, as the watch-dog, judicial organizations call the police to explain, it is not merely the credibility of the police, but also that of the pluralist ethic of the country that is at stake.

The image of the police in a metro city like Hyderabad is shaped, ironically by the drivers of the State Road Transport Corporation – an autonomous corporation, under the umbrella of the state government. The RTC drivers who are the users of public space called the roads along with other citizens, including pedestrians, who gravely violate all the traffic rules are not afraid of the police. It is the police who are afraid of the RTC drivers. The RTC drivers, the traffic police, and the citizens are all aware of this fundamental fact. All of them are also aware about the reasons for this acute phenomenon of Hyderabad. It makes a special case study in the disastrous management of traffic. The Public is in sympathy with the hapless constabulary. Several studies and reports have not helped the disastrous ground realities. It is this type of ground conditions that shape public opinion and their interface with the police.

The political malignancy, faulted federalism, regression of democracy, politically motivated deployment practices, and many similar factors external to police, matched by internal contradictions such as inadequacies of leadership, inadequate and at times 'proforma' training, hostile and adverse working conditions, discriminatory and differentiated standards and practices applicable to police personnel belonging to different organizations engaged in joint operations, lack of compulsory spells of rest, victimization and blame game, rather than protecting the police, working round-the-clock, under hostile conditions, often left in the lurch, deployment without back-up support, and a host of practices, contribute as causal and contributory factors of the police becoming a frustrated force in India.

A State Security Commission is not seen as a regulatory mechanism, as a buffer between the police and the political executive. What is more, it is often stated that the police leadership in India is accustomed to the 'security' of a political cover, as it helps explain away its own shortcomings in performance. In India, the political executive acts as the public relations functionary of the police, trying to defend and to explain away the shortcomings in performance. Some organizations, like the CRPF, the most dextrous force that has developed the ability to operate in diverse social situations, is perceived almost like a cheap labour force. Almost all states have conceded that the state police forces have become exposed to the political malignancies leading to both inefficiency and ineffectiveness. Democratic dissent and popular participation have assumed violent proportions and manifestations. Foul language has dominated democratic discourse in the face of provocative and violent actions and reactions.

Thanks to the skewed perceptions and practices in the name of human rights, the peace keeping, peace-making, conflict-resolution roles of the police have faded away. Planning and deployment decisions have gone out of police hands. Elected representatives and political executives on the one hand, and the judiciary on the other, have assumed a dominant role in its deployment, often on flimsy grounds. A senior police officer, a lady officer, perhaps for the first time, bluntly stated that, "police can't provide security for every individual, every temple or mosque." All this diffusion in the role of the police, high degree of partisan (direct and indirect) political control at the operational level, the expanded network of human rights institutions focusing on the police and policing practices, and most acutely, absence of a regulatory organization to facilitate autonomy and accountability are, at least to some extent, due to the commissions and omissions of the police leadership in protecting the police personnel, and organizations from these environmental and external factors.

The abuse of statutory powers apart from corrupt practices of a myriad nature, interjection by the political functionaries, powerful lobbies, and senior officers, in the honest performance of duty (by the book) at the police-station level, and traffic-management functions, all such interference happening in the full view of the pubic have shaped the stereotyped images of the police.

In the wake of statewide disturbances consequent upon the rape and murder of two women in the state of J & K (2009), the Home Minister of India promised to look into the withdrawal of the AFSPA, and gradual removal of troops from inhabited areas. He also promised, publicly, "to redraw the responsibilities among the forces." He elaborated that: "The Army is responsible for conventional defence at the borders, counter infiltration and counter terrorism within the state, while the paramilitary forces aid and assist the police in maintaining public order. Maintenance of law and order is the primary responsibility of the police."[33] That such basics of policing had to be reiterated by the Home Minister reveals the nature and extent of the mix-up between the Army, PMFs and the civil police. The role of 'para-military forces has not become any clearer. The respective roles cannot be confined to watertight compartments.

Encounter deaths, dragging alive an accused in a criminal case, tethered to a motor bike, in full view of the public and the media, an incident, which has happened in the state of Bihar, and many more similar incidents shape and defile police-public relations in India. These images acquire global fame when flashed by the media.

Although the orderly system was abolished several years ago, it was introduced through the back door by attaching constables for attending to telephone calls, receiving and delivering urgent messages, screening visitors and accompanying officers on tours. The constabulary were posted at the residences of political bosses and even retired police officers as a matter of privilege. For a long time, organizations have been able to ignore "externalities" – the side effects that their operations have on the society. But, as those ripple effects become more visible and measurable, the police leaders are waking up to the challenge of managing them.

Judicial strictures which are growing in frequency and intensity have not made much of an impact either on the political or on the police leadership. Such strictures can be ignored at the peril of efficacy and image of police organizations, and the democratic traditions of India. The polity has not only come to recognize, but is also going through a state of alarm that, as the Administrative Reforms (Veerappa Moily) Commission has observed, "Battle against crime can't be waged, much less won, without peoples' support, cooperation, a force pro-people but not pitted against."[34] Yet another commission headed by retired Justice D.N. Chowdhary (Assam), has observed "the police express rather low tolerance, the police misconduct, particularly unnecessary use of force and the use of abusive language."[35]

The People's War Group (PWG) had at one point rejected the laying down of arms as a condition imposed by the Government of Andhra Pradesh as a precondition for lifting the ban on the organization. Rejecting the condition, the PWG had maintained that the Government had no right to demand that an organization fighting for the downtrodden sections should not acquire weapons. Since the police repeatedly raid the villages in order to harass the poor, and because of the class interest, the State Government will not be able to direct the police to desist from all raids. People would have to arm themselves in order to resist police atrocities against the poor. The PWG had further stated that "restoration of discipline of the police and confidence of the people are the prime prerequisites for carving a positive image of the police. It is stated that if the choice is between 'democratic anarchy' and 'tranquility of a terrorist state', people prefer the former. As an adjunct, accountability to legislated norms is a *sine qua non* for building up and sustaining an image of state security organizations. But when they fail to nurture and project such an image of being apolitical and impartial, their efficacy and effectiveness get dented. Two former Presidents of India went on record stating that police organizations must cease to act in the style of agents of the political party in power.

Establishing public relations and cooperating with people have been reduced to the artificiality of a 'police-week' or a 'traffic week'. Today neither the citizens have respect for the police nor do the police respect the citizens. In the absence of discipline in the police and of confidence among the people, there can be hardly any cooperation between the two. Police leadership has a role and responsibility in establishing a cooperative relationship with the people. An important input into this process of establishing such a positive and cooperative equation between the two is to undertake a performance audit and report to the public periodically. Transparency and accountability will gain popular support to the police in fighting several battles, if only they desire and thus deserve. The initiative thus, not only for public cooperation, but also for securing support from the polity lies with the police, the police leadership.

Hostile community and police frustration are not two different, unrelated phenomena. They are intertwined, with a viscous reciprocal relationship of a cause and consequence. It is recognized that the people's role is crucial in preventing and/or containing terrorist attacks. It is not enough to recognize; That the common man has to be made a stake-holder. The concept of the 'public' should be appreciated as inclusive of the media. People and their groups have to be cultivated, co-opted as 'partners' having a stake in conflict and security management, and in police operations. The patriotic sentiment of citizens has to be protected, cultivated and utilized by the police. Police in India, which is projected as a peace force, a change agent of democratic social transformation is itself in dire need of change, a transformation, and also needs an image make-over.

4

Policy Reform: Dimensions : Dynamics : Directions

Policy reform in regard to post-independence policing in India can be scanned, scrutinized and some critical aspects crying for reform flagged. Some of these are: (a) the implications of the process of democratization of the Indian polity and the consequential demands on transformation of the police, attuning police to the changing democratic ethos of the polity. It is not just adjusting itself to the process of democratic transition, police have to make a positive contribution to democratic change as for e.g. not just protecting but, actively promoting human rights as a cardinal feature of democratization; (b) recognizing the (socio-economic political-cultural) change, and the (constitutional) vision for India, while attuning themselves (the police) consciously and effectively to such a shift in their goal, role, and style, with clarity; (c) promoting internalization and ensuring transparency in their functioning so as to promote and sustain democratic legitimacy as well as credibility in performance; (d) meeting the requirements of modernization not merely as a reaction to induction of technology by the hard-core criminals, extremists and terrorists, but in a proactive manner, and most important of all, (e) meeting the challenge of professionalization – attaining and maintaining standards of excellence in both organizational efficiencies and effectiveness in performance, thus enhancing the professional image as well as organizational productivity and excellence.

Democratization

Decentralization and Participation

Democratization, in the conceptual as well as India's contextual connotations means that all organizations have to operate as the instrumentalities of decentralization of organizational structures, and participatory ethos, both within the organization, as well as with reference to the demos, the people. It is indisputable that institutions in a democracy have to be 'people-centric', promoting peoples co-operation, not as 'subjects', but as the citizens. As citizens, even the police functionaries, are 'people' first, and police next. Peoples' participation is not merely 'desirable', but essential for the organizations to perform 'effectively'. That is the rationale for organizational transformation, attuning to the political transition from monarchy to democracy, people turning from 'subjects' to 'citizens'. Just as every organization represents an integral part of its environment, all organizations have to reflect the ethos of their environment. It is the collective responsibility of the organizations not merely to sustain but also to enhance the (democratic) quality of the society.

As the Indian polity had attained political freedom and moved on to becoming a constitutional Republic, and had commenced its journey encompassing socio-economic transformation, in tune with the constitutional vision (through the format of Five-Year Plans, beginning 1951), the polity had realized during 1985, i.e. seven Five-Year Plans later, that socio-economic transformation could not be realized as per design or to the full potential of Indian society, without peoples' participation. As a follow-up, we have affected two constitutional amendments (73rd and 74th) to facilitate decentralization and people's participation, as the twin pre-requisites for accelerating social transformation.[36]

Democracy the world over is taking a qualitative turn from the representative to the participative process. This is evident not only at the level of nation-states, but also reflected in small communities and social institutions, encompassing political, economic and social spheres. In spite of several distortions creeping in the 21st century is characterized by increasing degrees of democratic ethic, reflected in terms of literacy, awareness, empowerment and entitlements. There is a corollary, a parallel development, be it capitalist or socialist, south or north, east or west, all the nations are witnessing an ever increasing role of civil society in shaping and managing the socio-economic development and change. The institutions of state are also trying to shed off some of the functions hitherto being performed as a part of redefining and redesigning its role.

Decentralization of organizational structures facilitating participation by the people characterize the dynamic process of democracy. Decentralization takes in its canvas, vertical, horizontal and diagonal power shifts, as well as networking, and attunement of roles and goals. Two variables viz., (a) role-goal clarity, and (b) adequate and appropriate linkages that could harmonize, prove critical to the promotion and sustenance of decentralization. Decentralization and participation constitute not merely the facilitating factors of democratization in terms of a power shift, but are an integral part of democratic development, they are important measures of democracy. Inadequacies in the process of participation leads to alienation of the people towards an organization or towards the polity as the case may be. Democratization redefines the role of the state and warrants redesigning its structures and instrumentalities of state. Police are a vital part in sustaining the rule of law, integral to India's constitutional democracy

In sum and substance, participation itself is a necessary pre-condition to democratic development. Devoid of participation, both democracy and development tend to become centralized and authoritarian, getting distanced from people. Any movement away from the participative process negates both democracy and development – at all levels – a society, a community or an organization.

Initiation, promotion and sustenance of participation involve an organizational culture change, and constitute a function of leadership. Mahatma Gandhi contributed to such a culture by converting the freedom struggle into a freedom movement. This was successfully emulated, though in diverse situations and mutations, by Martin Luther King, Nelson Mandela, and (to an extent) Mikhail Gorbachev. There are many glaring, equally dramatic instances of culture change brought about at the level of organizations, in India. People's participation is like a high-yielding variety of seed; it flourishes under appropriate soil, water and fertilizer management.

Many a leader from police organizations, at different levels of hierarchy, in varying socio-economic conditions, had attributed deficiencies in the 'performance' of police, *inter alia*, to lack of (a) internal consultation and participation, and (b) 'cooperation' from the public. It can also be stated that where leadership did not facilitate but impeded participative culture within organizations, such leadership was isolated and denounced. Participative culture is a critical variable. It constitutes a motivational drive in the performance of organizations. A sense of 'withdrawal' and alienation represent the contra indicators of participation.

Democratic decentralization for policing, especially in the rural areas, have only recently assumed serious proportions because of the dynamic nature of society leading to the existing institutions of village administration becoming dysfunctional, due to extraneous factors that detracted from the common good of rural communities. Existing traditional institutions are being drawn into the vortex of partisan politicization. Institutional decentralization, like the Police Patel in the western states of India, or the Village Munisif in the southern states, or the Patwaris in eastern and northern India, could be restored and strengthened through re-engineering so as to suit the changing needs and contexts. The police are conscious of the fact that in view of developmental activities within the village, there is a need for agencies such as the Sarpanch Gram Sabha (Village Council), Nyaya Panchayats to work in concert with other agencies for the common good of communities. Renewal and rejuvenation of these institutions may also prove useful in countering partisan political factors. Such revival may also operate as an anti-dote to extremism. Institutional avenues already exist, they need to be revitalized in order to meet the changing needs and dynamics of decentralization.

Having a collective life as 'subjects' under a succession of kings, Nawabs, queens, Zamindars, be they benign or autocratic – a civilizational awakening has taken place all over the human society. India has taken a somewhat lead role in this transformation. Given the right leadership, this awakening triggered by the 'freedom movement' towards people's self-rule transformed people into citizens of the Republic. But, unfortunately, our growth-oriented 'development' has disrupted the life of grassroot, communities.

The contemporary police force in India was founded on the model of imperial police of British India that had its origins in the police force set up by Sir Charles Napier in the territory of Sindh in 1843, after the annexation of that territory. Napier patterned the organization after the Royal British. India had adopted the model based on a mix of the London Metropolitan Police Force and the older version of the Mughal system. The Police Commission, appointed by the alien ruler in 1860, had recommended the adoption, all over British India leading to the Police Act of 1861. Democratic India which had attempted police reform, *ad nauseam*, has yet to redefine, redesign and reengineer its police organizations and their functional ethos. British rule cannot be held an alibi; some critics comment that we would have been better off even if we had left the British system untouched.

Society, especially a democratic polity, undergoing the turbulence in an era of directed social change cannot afford to say that "police also, after all, is a part of the society and hence reflects all the contradictions and conflicts operating in the society". It is a mandated role of the leadership to infuse, sustain and promote the democratic ethic within their organizations. Police, especially after the initial decades (1950-80) is, sought to be recast as a part of the "agents of change" instead of remaining a mere "brute force" to maintain law and order. That's why, the budgetary allocations have been shifted to the category of planned "development" from the erstwhile division under the non-plan, "non-development" category.

The democratization of a police organization can be seen from diverse angles as indicated in Illustration 11.

Policing caste discrimination and conflict, caste-based politics, conflicts of religion, race, place of birth, residence, language etc,

Attributes of Democratic Development		Transformational Dispositions of Administrators	
		'Power'-centric	People-centric
1	– Demo-cenritic	– Autocratic – Prejudices – Corruption	– Authority as a trust – Integrity and honesty – Value reorientation – Rule of Law
3	– Citizen participation partnership	– Citizen distance Alienation – Hostile	– Peoples involvement – People as resource
6	– Result orientation	– Resistance to change – Supremacy of Rules, *per se* – Vested interests	– Innovation – Human Development – Upgradation of knowledge and skills
4	– Openness / Transparency – Freedom of / Access to information	– Confidentiality – Information as 'power' – Secretiveness	– Access to people – Access to information – Transparency
2	– Administrative decentralization	– Centralization – Hierarchical – Arbitrary exercise of power	– Participation – Team effort – Accountability
5	– Clarity of vision – Direction, Pace and process of change	– Inadequate commitment – Partisan / shifting alignments – Sabotage / collusion	– Commitment to social goals – Administrative neutrality – Espirit de crops
7	– Public Interest – Quality of life	– Partisan pursuits – Careerism	– Dedication to a cause – Public service – Professionalism

Illustration 11: Process of Democratic Transformation: Alternative Dispositions of Administrators

the need to make India a less unjust and non-exploitative society, call for imbibing the democratic spirit by the police first. The Indian police force has been recognized as a fair and efficient force, thus involved in several conflict zones of the global arena.

Decolonization of the 20th century is now being followed by several hitherto autocratic countries showing signs of assertive people-power and aggressive democratization leading to a more enduring consolidation of democracy; a changing environment which the police have to reckon with. It is in this background, intriguing to note that the police leadership was opposed to the legislative proposal and provision towards decentralization of police not as a part of but alongside the Panchayati Raj legislation in Karnataka. It gives an impression to the public that the police feel uncomfortable with even the prospect of working closely with the community. There is a democratic misalliance between the police and the polity.

Some autocratic leaders who usurped power in neighbouring countries, uncomfortable with India's success as a democracy, prompt infusion of fundamentalism and terrorism into and within India. The Prime Minister of India himself has set out some of the dimensions of external sources of threat thus: "Hostile groups and elements operating from across the border to perpetuate terrorist acts in India, where Jammu and Kashmir bears the brunt of the acts of these groups.[37] "Pakistan based terror groups constitute the "dark forces" opposed to India.[38] "The forces trying to divide society on communal lines, each one of these threats requires a strong effort, determination, hard work and continuous vigilance to tackle."[39]

The critical issues labeled variously as that of Maoism, Left Wing Extremism, and Naxalism, bring out the three dimensional challenges of managing extremism, law and order and democratic development. It has to be met by the political leadership ideologically, by the development administrators in terms of the process of social change, and law and order by the police, all at the same time. Towards this end, police have to develop their own 'think-tank' mechanism in order to explore and establish cooptative relations with the other organizations and attune their strategies to suit a democratic polity. It is easily said, but difficult to translate. The political leadership that argues that 'guns' do not solve the problem, shift their disposition after assuming power by stating at times that guns are inevitable. Many a liberal citizen of India welcome the reported decision of the Government of Rajasthan to 'shoot at sight' poachers of tigers. Democracy cannot afford to be reduced to lawlessness.

The political process alone legitimizes social change by securing popular endorsement and participation. Yet, the malignancies of politicization can distort the balance of power. Thus, there is a need to distinguish two types of politicization, the benevolent (and legitimate), and the partisan (and thus malignant). Benevolent is what obtains nearest to the people The two types are mutually incompatible, but we often find a combination of the two. If the malignancies predominate, the political process degenerates and democracy gets distorted or even destroyed. It is in such a context of (role) conflict, that during the 1970s Lok Nayak Jaya Prakash Narayan issued a call to the police asking them not to act on the 'undemocratic' and 'illegal' directions of the political parties and partisan orders of governments.

Political process in its benevolent mode represents the process of harmonization of diverse values, interests and identities operating in any society, Benevolent politicization is a vital prerequisite for societies to maintain stability ('continuity') and to promote change. It helps retain the gravity of democracy within the society. Occasional demands by sections of people for a military rule, a second constitution, presidential form of government, or, a reference to the British rule as more responsive and less corrupt, illustrate the popular perceptions of the levels of the malignant politicization in post-independence India. Indian society had seen the best and worst manifestations of democracy viz., the consensual mode of 'sculpting' the constitution proclaimed in 1950, and the conflict mode of 'working' their democracy, which could slide into anarchy.

The beauty of the democratic political process, in all societies, is that it pressures all institutions, ultimately, to restore legitimacy through peoples' endorsement and credibility with people-centric service. The modus and time frame for securing such a renewal is determined by specific conditions obtaining in a society at any given point of time. In the Indian context, 'Emergency' as a political malignancy could not last for more than two years. Renewal and legitimization of the political process in India is more glaringly illustrated by the 'stability' of democracy. True and more democracy is thus the best remedy for the ills of democracy. There is an ever increasing recognition by political parties that people matter, in their responsive performance and accountability. It is also being experienced by the political parties, true to the adage that "you can fool all the people for some time, and some people for all times but not all the people for all times". Benevolent political process is the best safety valve in any society, whilinge malignancy of the process if allowed to persist for long, could prove cancerous, and even worse. Conflict and violence may exist in a democracy. In fact, democracy generates some level of conflict, but when conflict becomes violent, and crosses the 50:50 ratio into 49:51, it can destroy democracy. It would then be a matter of time to regenerate democratic order.

What about the other, mainline and prime instrumentalities of state viz., the executive (including police) and the judiciary? The credibility of the judiciary in India is at a low ebb. It is showing signs of awareness of its own problems such as (a) low level of performance and (b) loss of credibility. Its response is positive as illustrated by the emergence of Public Interest Litigation, *Lok Adalats* and *Praja Courts* but yet it is slow and inadequate. The judiciary has yet to recognize the magnitude of its negative image and sliding credibility as is made evident by two facts. For every one case docketed (staggering numbers, no doubt) there is at least one dispute not preferred by the public, for the public is aware that their problems may not be resolved during their lifetime, and if it is resolved, the process could prove more frustrating and costly in the 'judicial casinos', as the first citizen, the President of India has put it, in a Golden Jubilee overview. A more glaring evidence of the loss of credibility and the need for renewal of judicial institutions is that people are tending to take the law into their own hands. The law and Order scenario represents a case of institutional bypass. It is said that what one sees depends upon where one sits. The judiciary in India looks at itself, and thinks it has a 'full-view' of itself. It rejects any 'outsider' view, peoples view, as 'inadmissible', and 'contemptuous'.

The democratic credibility and legitimacy of the executive, in sum and substance, is characterized by an ever-growing distance between the citizen and the administrator, and increasing degrees of alienation and mutual hostility. The administrator is assigned the role of a change agent, by the polity. But an overview of administration (including that of police), obtaining today can be stated just in one sentence. It is the image, credibility and low performance of the administration, and alienation, if not hostility, between the citizen and the administrator that is reflected on the electoral fortunes of the political parties in India. 'Anti-incumbency' represents a public stricture against the administration, not merely on the political party. The political parties admit it. The administrators do not refute it openly.

The administration cannot remain untouched by the democratic process or politicization of the benevolent type. Administration cannot for all times run parallel to, but has to run along with the people. Participation integrates and harmonizes the police and the people. As the adage goes, no society is immune to the eternal process of change. As social change is eternal, no institution within any given society can remain static. All institutions seek to influence the environment within which they operate, and attune themselves to the changing environment as a constant process. Without this elixir of change, societies and organizations stagnate, decay and slip into civilizational oblivion. Institutions lose their functional relevance, get atrophied, become objects of archaeology, a part of history. History is replete, and testifies to organizational (a) atrophy, as well as (b) transformation, keeping in tune with the transitions of historical time-frames in any society.

Police have remained relatively static in a 'world of change' that has taken place and is taking place in India. People have fought a century-long 'war without violence', won 'freedom', and as "we the people" set out a national vision through a consensual democratic process, like never before. No institution can operate in India outside the constitutional frame; all have to work together in order to remain legitimate and credible. What is this vision of India, as envisioned in the Constitution, recognized the world ever as the best and most comprehensive document on human rights?

> WE THE PEOPLE OF INDIA, having solemnly resolved to constitute India into a **SOVEREIGN SOCIALIST SECULAR DEMOCRATIC REPUBLIC** and to ensure to all its citizens:
> **JUSTICE**, social, economic and political.
> **EQUALITY** of status and of opportunity; and to promote among them all
> **FRATERNITY** assuring the dignity of the individual and the unity and integrity of the nation;
> IN OUR CONSTITUENT ASSEMBLY this twenty-sixth day of November, 1949, do HEREBY ADOPT, ENACT AND GIVE TO OURSELVES THIS CONSTITUTION.

It is in this canvas and the vision of India, that the stakes of all the stake holders shaping the mission of the police in India has been formulated by a group of officers of the Indian Police Service as presented in Illustration 12.

Keeping all the stake holders and their stakes, the group of police officers had formulated the mission of police in India.[39] as follows:

The MISSION

> Commitment to and promotion and protection of the values and goals enunciated by the Constitution of India, maintaining independent image and role as an instrument of the state, preserving the legitimacy of government, promoting faith in law, protecting the sanctity of rule of law and promoting security, peace and harmony in society, ensuring the enjoyment of protective discrimination extended by the state to the weaker sections; maintenance of essential services, preservation of national integrity, ensuring due process and an expeditious, fair-trail on apprehending the culprits, with an outgoing disposition towards the citizens so as to promote healthy and cooperative relations with citizens – thus contributing to the mission of improving the human condition in society, and, in order to do that, constantly developing and attuning own organizational structures and ethos as well as human resources in a manner as to be able to influence and fulfill public policy and win over public confidence.

	Stakeholders	Their stakes
1	Citizens	– Protection of rights – Prevention of crime – Effective apprehension of culprits & punishment – Peace, sense of security – Honesty fair play and civility
2	Weaker sections	Protective discrimination
3	Tourists / Visitors	Civility, safety and security
4	Public Interest Groups	Commitment in promoting their interests
5	Accused	Expeditious & fair prosecution
6	Convicts	Humane treatment & reform
7	Extremists	Democratic space for their ideological stance
8	Political parties	Protection of vested interest Affirmation to partisan interests and ideology
9	Political executive	Support for their programmes
10	Legislatures	Strict legality
11	Government	Conformity to, and Compliance with policies
12	Judiciary	– Conformity with Law; – Processual Justice
13	Lawyers	– Professional role – Professional avocation
14	Industry	– Protection of property – Curb on industrial unrest and violence
15	Police (a) Top	– Image, autonomy – Involvement in policy formulation
	(b) Middle	– Sense of involvement in the management – Operational / autonomy / commensurate with responsibility
	(c) Field	– Role / Goal clarity – Operational support – Adequate working conditions – Promotional opportunities

Illustration 12: Stake Holders and Stakes

Indeed, framing a mission statement for police organizations is not the exclusive task of the police but that of society as well, all the stake holders. It has to evolve as a memorandum of understanding (MoU), where the police had to play a lead role. It is a process, laborious but creative and fascinating. The one presented here is the result of police officers deliberating and drafting in just about three hours; a commendable effort.

Irrespective of time and space, the roots of all institutions/ organizations (political, economic, social or cultural) can be traced to the dynamics of the society. The emergence, continued existence, survival (with fluctuating fortunes), and ultimately the evolution and / or extinction of institutions are influenced by the performance of organizations. Institutions that fulfill the mission assigned to them derive support from and appreciation of the society. Those that prove deficient in performance are rejected to varying degrees.

The process of appreciation or depreciation of organizations by the public depends upon: (1) the dynamics of social change, and demands of change on the organizations, (2) the nature and degree of cooptation among the multiplicity of institutions having common objectives and complementary tasks, (3) identification of the diverse stakeholders and their stakes; (4) constant harmonization of competing stakes on a normative basis; (5) recognition of complementarities in their mission, objectives and roles; and (6) cooptation among institutions with the aid of appropriate systems, professional standards and codes of ethics. Thus, identification of the diverse stake-holders and their stakes constitutes a critical process towards the fulfillment of the vision and mission, culminating in attaining levels of organizational excellence.

No society, not even a small tribal community, in a remote area, remains stagnant or stable, for, 'change' is the only constant in any society. Changes in any society can be looked at from diverse angles. An overview suggests that factors of change can be seen as falling into three streams, running in several directions and at a variable pace. The three sets of factors may be labeled as (a) values (e.g. democracy, gender justice, human rights et al), (b) socio-economic conditions (e.g., 'land to the tiller', 'economic liberalization', 'subsidies' et al, and (c) technological (eg. Infm.

Tech, CCTV, AK47, unmanned stealth aircraft, et al). These three sets of factors may not flow parallel or at the same pace, or even in the same direction. The pattern may be akin to tributaries of a mighty river system, several tributaries merging into the mainstream, and again branching off, in diverse direction, and ultimately confluence with the oceans.

In all societies, nations, communities and even in the smallest unit of 'organization, viz. a family, diversity is a phenomenon that leads to competition and conflict of values, interests and identities (gender equality, dowry, discrimination against girl-child *et al*). All organizations, in all societies, are created by the society in order to subserve its demands. It is the function of every such organization to take cognizance of the competing and conflicting demands made on it. It has to negotiate with the society, and the complementary institutions, and harmonize the stakes of the various stake-holders, in formulating the mission assigned. For eg., when political parties/leaders demand 'security' for all religious places it is as a part of this MoU that such issues have to be got clarified. In the context of the frequent attacks on churches in Karnataka, the government said it was difficult to provide security for all places of worship and suggested that the managements of religious institutions make necessary arrangements for security. The Minister for Home Karnataka state, [V.S. Acharya] had stated it was extremely difficult to provide police protection at all places of worship. "There are 1.25 crore houses, 43,000 temples, 3,000 mosques and churches in the State. The State has only 90,000 police personnel and it is difficult to provide security to all places", and individuals.

Organization and Management

Given the prime characteristic that police in India have not transformed themselves to meet the demands of political transition to and to the process of democracy, how far and how well have the police 'organized' themselves to meet the new and emerging demands from the polity? In the face of expanding role and increasing load, police response has been seen in terms of tremendous growth in numbers and range of police forces since the beginning of democratic era. The growth can be summed up as numerical but not adequately matched by enhancement in the 'organizational' efficiencies and effectiveness. On the contrary, growth in numbers has led to significant increases in the levels of hierarchy and imbalances in the 'head' to 'tail' ratios. It can also be stated that democratic development and rapid growth in the overall size of police represent a mutually negating process. Organizational proliferation has led to role-goal dissonance both within and between the police forces. Indian polity has excelled itself in the creation of 'new' organizations and structural changes (tinkering may be a more appropriate description), more on an *ad hoc* basis, from time to time. The consequences are many such as for e.g. (a) proliferation of levels – the organizational bulge – has resulted in the fragmentation of the span of roles, leading to 'higher' designations but diminished span, authority and accountability leading to job dissatisfaction; (b) increasing levels, functionally and territorially, which should have resulted in 'decentralizaiton' which is mismatched on the ground, by modernization and upgradation of 'on-line' communication systems leading to centralization of command and control, making redundant the several middle tiers thus (c) demoralizing the police due to 'level-jumping' especially within the higher levels of hierarchy. The organizational game is also fouled by the diagonal relationships of 'control' by the political party cadres as well as elected representatives such as the MLA and the MP in regard to the functioning of the police.

The situation is made more complex as between the different police organizations, civil, armed, CPOs and PMFs in regard to deployment and operational networking, where multiple forces are deployed in all types of operations in varying patterns, often on publicly debated perceptions of 'performance' deficiencies of the local police. There has emerged a hierarchy, somewhat akin to the Indian caste system, among the different police forces in India. As adverted earlier, civil police has been attuned, used and misused to meet political, partisan ends, and denounced by some of the respected, venerable Chief Ministers. While Chief Ministers and Home Ministers at the state level had seen the Central Reserve Police

Force (CRPF) as equivalent to 'cheap labour' (for it comes without a financial burden), its deployment had been seen as an integral part of the 'political' process by the Centre, in the context of Article 356 of the Constitution. Size or volume and timing of deployment, nature of operational involvement, duration, phasing and pattern of withdrawal are determined by the Union government, not on the basis of a professional assessment of the situations either by the civil police at the state level, or any professional assessment and appraisal of the situations by the directorates of the CPOs/PMFs. The deployment of PMFs in internal, civilian situations of turbulence was on occasions, ostensibly aimed at providing them with opportunities of experience, but more substantially, such deployment of units had been resorted to—due to pressures for relief from the 'monotonous' nature of their duties on the borders. In fact, there is a clear mismatch between the training imparted and equipment acquainted by the CPOs and the nature of skills needed to be able to participate in 'internal' situations of turbulence. Irrespective of the efficacy of such a mix of diverse forces in civilian disturbances, the civil police are totally demoralized. The central forces are deployed to aid and assist the civil police, but in reality, the CPOs had assumed a posture of superiority in status and skills, and thus assumed a higher level of self-esteem in their equations with the civil police. The inter-se role clarity as between the CPOs (& PMFs) vis-à-vis civil police continue to remain hazy, leaving a disastrous impact on the police organizations as a whole. A deeper analysis reveals that the several forces – civil, CPOs and PMFs and their diverse units are not oriented adequately for any kind of joint operations.

The Indian polity has excelled itself in tinkering with the organizational structures and deployment patterns of the police forces. Adhocism is the name of the game. Reform of the police has been reduced to structural tinkering or creation of new structures, but not in any comprehensive fine-tuning of the police network, or police work. The political parties, almost all of them, all the time have been accustomed to using and abusing the police as the handmaid of partisan politics. That is why, any and every new Chief Minister starts with a 'total' shake-up of the police almost as his / her first task soon after assuming the office as Chief

Minister. And, the police leadership has not taken any initiative to get rid of this 'Jugular-grip' of political leaders over the police. It has its disastrous impact on the entire police force, at all levels. This situation has, what prompted a senior police officer to say, "We are professionals but working for unprofessional organizations." The political system continues to take full advantage of the situation, inspite of public interest litigation prompted judicial dicta directing operational autonomy for and matching accountability of the police. On their part, several Home Ministers (at the level of the states) have been seen operating as the public relations executives of the police, defending the police, perhaps as a *quid pro quo*, and thus containing the onslaught of 'opposition' parties in the legislatures. Structurally, the most critically operational unit of police organizations viz. the police station, and its chief functionary viz., the Station House Officer, are so enervated that they have become the weakest links between the citizens and the police in India.

It may be noted that the 'structure' of any organization need not be, should not be, perceived as sacrosanct, for they are only a means to an end. It is a trite saying that organizations are only as good as the people who man and manage them.

Indians in general are considered high on knowledge levels and well equipped with the skills, thus highly 'capable'. But, inspite of such high levels of capability, they are poor performers under Indian socio-political ground conditions. In the context of the police in India, capabilities are unquestionable, but motivational deficit caused by a multiplex of factors is a reality.

Analytical Elements of organizational Performance :					
K	Knowledge	S	Skills	C	Capability
V	Values	A	Attitudes	M	Motivation
C	Capability	M	Motivation	P	Performance

The Indian Mujahideen came to light after the [Feb 23], 2005, blast in Varanasi, as a shadow outfit of the banned Students Islamic

Movement of India (SIMI) and the Pakistan-based terrorist outfit, Lashker-e-Taiba. This reality has been reinforced by many other terrorist attacks, such as in Bangalore, Ahmedabad and New Delhi, during 2008. Intelligence agencies suspected and believed that the SIMI was also operating as a front group of the notorious Pakistani terrorist group Harkat-ul-Jihad-al Islami (HUJI). In yet another terrorist attack in Pune (German Bakery) a sleeper cell was suspected to be involved. It was not until (June) 2010, that the Union Government has declared the Indian Mujahideen (IM) a shadow outfit of the banned (SIMI) and Pakistan based Lashkar-e-Taiba, a long established terrorist organization. Questions arise in this background as to how stringent is the Unlawful Activities (Prevention) Act, 1967, and how stringent (or to be more precise, how lax) is the action under the law? Also such lax action in the case of terrorist outfits, and equally lax political reaction emerge as a disturbing trend and as a factor of police demoralization.

Apart from these gaps between the law and its implementation in regard to extremist and terrorist organizations, and watering down of the changes, as for example in the Bhopal gas disaster, from culpable homicide to a one on-par with a road accident, at the instance of the then Chief Justice of India, a cardinal question of 'transparency' arises. The secrecy of information in the public domain, the sealed reports of a countless commissions and committees, the multiple layers and tiers of enquiries into the same incident, such as the Godhara train tragedy – all of them, constitute acts of concealment of facts from the public, raising the issue of transparency as a democratic imperative, and informed public participation in public affairs. What to disclose, how much, at what stage and at what level, and similar questions are not given adequate consideration keeping in view operational nuances, an aware citizenship, and the morale and motivation of the security forces. No polity, especially a democracy can afford to demoralize its security forces. "There is a lack of institutional coordination and direction in national security matters, ... agencies had developed a culture of managing information in a manner designed to protect their individual institutional interests".... the consequences of such efforts to deny intelligence to the police resulting in an "impoverished response to terrorist threats". "Government agencies were in possession of significant pieces of information that taken together, would have led a competent analyst to conclude that Flight AI 182 was at high risk of being bombed by a known Sikh terrorist, in June 1985".[41]

"Distortions of the political processes seep through the network of institutions and the processes of governance. When the 'political-will' and the national vision are blurred, the 'administrative-will' and its mission get blunted. When the political process puts the 'partisan' as a priority, the administrative process gets corrupted, reduced to careerism, gradually snow-balling into collusion, derailing both democracy and development". "Enervation and decimation of the institutions of governance by an administration resistant to reform leads to loss of efficacy, effectiveness, accountability and credibility. Popular unrest assumes the form of confrontation between the citizens and the state. In its attempt to 'contain' unrest instead of addressing the root causes and problems (land reforms, exploitation, discrimination) state finds it 'convenient' to convert socio-economic issues into problems of law and order. Solutions are perceived and pursued in directions such as adding battalions to police organizations, and draconian laws. As socio-economic problems cannot be resolved through the intervention of police forces, not equipped to deal with the complexity of the situation, police tend to resort to what they are adept at, viz., excessive and extended use of draconian laws, third degree methods, lock-up and encounter deaths, all these snowballing into problems of human rights and state terrorism".[42]

Police try to tackle the illegitimate consequences such as communal, political and social disturbances and distortions emerging from the process of mal-governance. In addition to losing many lives fighting extremists and terrorists, police end up with a poor image and widespread demoralization.

As the National Human Rights Commission (NHRC) of India has observed, "While the restoration of peace may indeed be the *sine qua non* for the full respect of human rights, timely and sagacious political measures that are truly democratic in character are necessary, as in the long run, they have far more lasting and beneficial results than reliance essentially on security forces, however devoted and disciplined they are, or on restrictive laws, however carefully they may be applied."[43] Strengthening the democratic ethic is the only weapon perhaps in the war against anti-democratic forces. Adverting to police organizations which are admittedly in crying need of reform, the NHRC pinpointed that, "In almost all parts of the country there is a clear and increasing need to reform the police itself, to retrain and to reorganize it and to restore to it the skills and the integrity that the country so desperately needs if the function of preserving law and order is to be improved."[44] Reform measures can't be dragged over decades; at best, they can be stretched to months. The agenda should be entrusted to a police leadership with an unbroken spell of tenure.

We have Chief Ministers making serious allegations against the Centre, on the floor of state assemblies, of hatching a conspiracy to pull down the state governments, asking people to "carry arms", and to beat up "corrupt administrators". People may not have acted on such advice, but they have not protested against such counsel either. An emerging and rather an alarming trend is the element of partisan bias attributed to the police in the apprehension of alleged criminals. This could set a trend leading to the dangerous proportions of demanding a 'quota' system in criminal investigations whereby the proportion of criminals should be proportionate to the ratio of different sections in the population. The demands for a 'minority' police are assuming serious proportions, though such a prescription could only aggravate the disease of 'bias'. Instead of resolving or at least containing conflict and violence in the society it may end up with police fighting police.

Distortions of democracy may prove to be a slippery path for the police if police don't negotiate their role with the polity. There can be political turmoil as in Nepal, Bangladesh, Egypt and many other countries. Nearer home, in India, aggressive police entering the court halls of the Madras High Court, presiding officers summoning civil police into the precincts of legislatures to aid and assist the Marshals, police beating unarmed people, accused persons being dragged on the roads tethered to their motor cycles, molestation of women in distress visiting seeking police help and many more such aberrations creep into the system turning democracies into anarchies and mobocracies. It is noteworthy that within two days of Hosni Mubarak making way for democracy, the Egyptian police came on to the streets agitating for corrections to their image and credibility sullied by their role against the people agitating against Hosni Mubarak. In India, it has taken ten years before they came out, motivated sanguinely, or politically.

The role of the leadership of police organizations, or units thereof, is to negotiate and assume either generic or situation-specific 'objectives', and roles. Exposed to a high level of political malignancies, the police units are asked first to rush to trouble spots, as directed by either the political bosses, or civil administration without an adequate appreciation of the nature of the problem (communal tensions, caste-conflict, political turmoil, mass-upsurge, extremist or terrorist violence). CPOs are generally involved in a professional assessment of the nature, magnitude and complexity of the problem. On many an occasion, as if to demonstrate administrative hierarchy and authority, CRPF units are despatched / airlifted without any briefing on the nature of the problem, or professionally tuned operational norms, which would help avoid *post-facto ad hoc* pronouncements like: "police should have exercised maximum restraint", "render full protection to the people", and worse, condemning CPO units, that are trained to aid and assist civilian police, but not assume direct charge of situations, or, control over the civil police. Rushing (a company of 100) soldiers from the specialized Combat Battalion for Resolute Action (COBRA), where CRPF units are already operating, perhaps represents a measure of incoherence in strategic decision-making, in ways more than one, such as (a) the nomenclature of COBRA suggests that other forces are not resolute, or not allowed to be, to the same degree, (b) Image distortions, leading to (c) projection of a hierarchy among the police forces, making cooptation difficult in joint operations. There need not be statutory provisions to undertake self-appraisal of organizational performance. It can be undertaken as a periodic audit and published in order to promote awareness among the public. It can assume the form of a 'social audit' by any civil society professional organization, or performance audit in addition to any other form of departmental or statutory audit. Such an audit can provide an opportunity to correct the image distortions of the police in society, and can also generate public pressure to secure a correct, appropriate and adequate policy support from the polity. Any and every form of audit promotes transparency.

It is not the creation of new organizations and deployment of a multiplicity of organizations in joint operations that is important, but the working of existing organizations that is critical to the police image and efficacy. This is what Justice B. Sudarshan Reddy, Judge of the Supreme Court, observed while hearing a writ petition filed by one of the former Union Law Ministers, Ram Jethmalani in the case of Hasan Ali Khan, involving black money stashed in foreign banks. Justice Sudarshan Reddy observed: "No further information is coming out. Only one individual is here. What about others? It is very difficult to be calm and quiet after seeing the status report. Why were all agencies sleeping since 2008? Why has it (Enforcement Directorate) moved only after this Court stepped in? If this writ petition had not been filed nothing would have happened". Justice Sudarshan Reddy told the Solicitor General, "why no question is asked about the source of income. This is the first step in the investigation. What is coming in the way of going to the root of the matter? National security angle still remains unanswered."[44]

An appropriate appraisal would enhance the ability of the police to be able to appreciate futuristic scenarios of security problems and the proactive role of the police – such as cybercrimes and new-generation weapons of terrorists. Performance of all organizations necessarily depends upon the existence of an organizational think-tank within, to be able to think and act in a proactive manner and prepare in good time in order to be able to nip emerging problems in the bud. Deterrence is the name of the game.

Promotion of appropriate values and attitudes conducive to the performance of organizations is a critical function of leadership. Awards, rewards and punishments in a transparent manner, also a function of leadership, plays a critical role in promoting and sustaining high levels of morale and thus of motivation, leading to fructification of capabilities of the human resources. Any misappropriation of awards and rewards could be disastrous to the morale of a whole police force, as has been witnessed often in India. It is in this canvas, that we have to examine the intent and content of 'public' appeals, by the political parties, elected 'representatives' and administrators 'appealing' for 'public cooperation', and appeals to the media not to publish full facts of the events, knowing well that the public must know facts and ground conditions for them to be able to participate in well informed public discourse, which will help public policy and follow-up action. Indeed, in several countries, in contemporary times, public opinion and its articulation (even if archestrated) are projected and used as strong factors in shaping public policy. Self-proclaimed groups of intelligentia occasionally sprout dishing out 'opinions' on public issues without an adequate appreciation of the true meaning and role of intellectualism in society. In a society characterized by motivated criticism, informed public opinion is a critical ingredient to protect the positive image of police organizations.

In the Indian context, police organizations and leaders shy away from expression of their own professional/organizational views on the several issues of security, public policy and the role of the police. Police initiatives in sectarian matters can create ripples in society, or even aggravate social tensions. This was illustrated in a report by Mahim Pratap Singh, in *The Hindu* covering a police order for profiling the Christian population in Madhya Pradesh following which the ruling BJP party found itself entangled in the controversy. The report stated thus:

> "The March 22, 2011 Order was issued by the office of the Senior Superintendent of Police, Bhopal and instructed station in-charge officers to gather details about "activities of Christians. "An internal probe headed by the Additional Director General of Police (Intelligence R.K. Shukla) has been ordered by the Police Department to find out who issued the controversial order. "The order seeking

meticulous details of Catholic and Protestant members of the Christian community at the District and Tehsil levels was subsequently withdrawn following protests from Christians.

"The details sought include the number of Christian missionaries, amount of foreign aid received by them, criminal elements associated with Christian organizations and the political protection available to them, convent schools with details of enrolled students, sensitive Christian populated areas with details of people's percentage wise economic status and their income sources.

"However, neither Shivraj Singh Chauhan nor higher police officials had any knowledge about where the order came from.

"The order was issued by someone at the junior levels, without my knowledge. It was not meant to target any community in particular, and the intention was to get these details for better service to the Christians in the State, Director General of Police S.K. Raut told *the Hindu* who also maintained that "as of now, the order stands withdrawn and no such details will be gathered.

"The Christian community in the state has been enraged by the order. The Archbishop of Bhopal Leo Cornelio has stated that there seems to be a sinster plan behind all this, and if the CM and other officials say that they are not aware, it is all the more shocking. If it is not someone inside the government, the government should apologise and if not it should find out and punish the culprit. This is clear targeting and profiling of the minority community and a violation of the Constitution and principles of a free and fair democracy. The Archbishop further asked why the police would go about gathering these details right after the national census during which all relevant details have already been recorded.

"The CPI(M) State Secretary Badal Saroj asked if there is a secret RSS Cell within the police headquarters in Bhopal, and maintained that merely revoking the order is

> not enough, and that the Government should name those behind this and take action against them."[46]

A variety of reasons can be adduced for this phenomena; but the consequences are (a) when the police leadership express a view, rarely, is it reacted to aggressively as 'motivated' and thus unacceptable and untenable, (b) The public in our democracy is deprived of the opinion and professional wisdom of the police, (c) The public is guided by a set of partisan prejudices and stereotypes in the absence of verifiable facts and tenable explanations, (d) Prolonged silence of professional (police) leaders on public issues prompts some political leaders to state that police leadership should not make statements of public policy. Promoting awareness is a *sine qua non* in democracy to secure its enrichment, rejuvenation and renewal.

The adverse impact of political malignancy on the police has led to a widespread perception among the middle and lower levels of police organizations, a perception of helplessness, and indifference on the part of their own leadership, in turn distorting the police-public relations into one of hostility. In such a situation, when people tend to take law into their own hands, violence and conflict assume untenable levels for a democratic polity. India today represents a violent democracy. Even if the police is not responsible for this state of affairs, it is their responsibility to explain, contain, control and manage violence.

A police force, disillusioned by its own leadership, and frustrated as a consequence of realization of their low-levels of efficacy and social acceptability, is tending to take their frustration upon the citizens, manifest in forms such as (a) aggressive and violent police action assuming the proportions of 'police-*raj*', (b) 'contrived encounters' and (c) lock-up deaths. The situation is also characterized by a sense of 'withdrawal' reflected in forms of suicides, and indiscriminate shoot-outs of citizens as well as colleagues and officers within the force. A glaring piece of empirical evidence of police helplessness is that in Hyderabad the police are afraid of RTC drivers, where the RTC drivers are not only not afraid of but look down upon the police with contempt.

And the police recognize that the citizens are aware of the nature of police helplessness. State terrorism is a disputed issue, widely debated, but police frustration and violence are not disputed in India today. When police morale goes down very low; it is not good for the police and their organization, certainly not congenial for a democratic polity.

Inspired by the ideals of the 'freedom movement', Indian leadership, right from Jawaharlal Nehru to Manmohan Singh, have held the supremacy of human rights, set up a chain of Human Rights Commissions, at the level of both states and the nation, inspite of the fact that the Judiciary in India, especially the Supreme Court and the High Courts, had upheld and expanded the rights of jurisprudence and jurisdiction substantially. Prime Minister Manmohan Singh had reiterated even in the context and vortex of Jammu and Kashmir, zero tolerance for human rights violations. Yet, even under the normative standards of zero tolerance, the institutions of governance, especially those working for the protection and promotion of human rights, indulge in violations against unarmed civilian populations after affixing labels such as 'informants', 'operatives', 'ideologues', and 'sympathizers', of extremist organizations. The Police have an excellent opportunity to redefine their role in promoting human rights awareness and protection in place of the existing scenario of police as the transgressors of human rights of specific groups, in diverse situations.

Police organizations in India have come to suffer an 'image distortion' and are placed at the receiving end. All other institutions in the pantheon have arrogated to themselves a higher pedestal and simultaneously edged the civil police to lower echelons. The police have not articulated, asserted or manoeuvred adequately for a place of parity if not for a higher order, on the basis of their complex, delicate, multiple role-set. They allowed themselves to remain in an antiquated status and role profile. While 'serving' the partisan interests of the political parties, they have not been able even to bargain for any *quid pro quo* to their organizations. Such partisan dispositions of the police had at best secured momentary advantages to the police leadership at the expense of the image and credibility of police organizations. This is a major factor for the demoralization of the police, adversely affecting their performance, and their image among the public. A demoralized team cannot play the game, certainly not according to the rules. In such a situation, public hostility and police frustration acquire a state of viscious and cyclical relationship. It seems that in the Indian context the public is more conscious and concerned about the need for strengthening the police organizations and police personnel. Police frustration is vividly reflected, in their conduct, and performance of their role, in the form of police brutalities. The Public is aware that when the political leaders, as policy makers, do not take appropriate care of the police, the frustrated police revolt, which is very dangerous to the constitutional democratic fabric of the society. Alas, the much needed State (National) Security Commission would have taken appropriate initiatives of policing the police.

The police have demonstrated, consistently, that they do not like to 'co-operate' with the public. Where positions of authority are not seen as public trust, but seen as power per se, as authority, to be utilized not in the interest of the public but appropriated for private purposes, unjust ends. There emerges a contempt of citizens. Democratic empowerment and peoples' participation are edged out and their powers are misappropriated by the administration through the process of centralization. Constitutional decentralization has been negated by bureauçratic centralization. Centralization with a built-in authoritarianism has become the cardinal ground reality impeding accountable performance of the police organizations.

The concept of a 'State Security Commission' is more than 30 years old. The National Police Commission (NPC), headed by Dharma Vira in its report submitted to the Government of India in 1980, has recommended the setting up of such a Commission in all the states with a view to promoting the 'organizational autonomy' of police and 'accountability in performance' within the framework of the law. Pointing out the gross dilution of such accountability, and its implication for our parliamentary democracy, the National Police Commission quoted the observations of the

Shah Commission, in its Third and Final Report: [6 August 1978: Paras 24.10 and 24.17) thus:

> "The political system that our Constitution has given to our country is such that it contemplates parties with different political ideologies administering the affairs of the Centre and the State Governments. It is necessary in the interest of the territorial, political and economic integrity of the nation to ensure that the factors which contribute to such integrity are forever and continuously strengthened and not impaired. One such factor, and a very important and decisive one, is the body of public servants at various levels and particularly those at the decision-making levels belonging to the different disciplines and functioning in the states and the Centre. If the basic unity and territorial integrity of the country is to be emphasized at the political level it is imperative to ensure that the officials at the decision making levels are protected and immunized from threats or pressures so that they can function in a manner in which they are governed by one single consideration – the promotion of public well-being and the upholding of the fundamentals of the Constitution and the rule of law. The Government ought to ensure this if necessary, by providing adequate and effective safeguards to which the officials may turn if and when necessary against any actual or attempted threats by the political and / or administrative authorities to sway the officials from performance of their legitimate duties."
>
> ". . . . . The system must be overhauled with a view to strengthen it in a manner that the functionaries working the system do so in an atmosphere free from the fear of the consequences of their lawful actions and in a spirit calculated to promote the integrity and welfare of the Nation and the rule of law. This will call for considerable heart-searching both at the political and the administrative levels. Both the groups, during the period of the emergency, sadly deviated from their respective legitimate roles of

duty, trespassing into each other's areas with the consequences that are there for all to see and many to lament. If the officials on the one side and the politicians on the other do not limit their areas of operation to their accepted and acknowledged fields, this Nation cannot be kept safe for working a democratic system of Government ......"

After thus clarifying the basic premise of autonomy and matching accountability, the National Police Commission [NPC] made its observations and recommendations on setting up a State Security Commission (SSC) in each state. Some of the observations and recommendations of the NPC demand a detailed consideration.

A. Government's Superintendence over Police

The National Police Commission observed that the phenomenon of 'interference' with the functioning of the police, in popular estimate and belief, is linked with the existing system of control over the police by the political executive in the Government. Referring to the arguments that the Ministers in charge of police have to account for and defend police performance in the state legislatures, and in order to fulfill this responsibility properly the Home Ministers must have full control over the police and that police cannot be conceived as an agency independent of government control, the National Police Commission (NPC) observed that while attempting to insulate the police from unauthorized interference from political and other extraneous sources, a system has to be devised in which the police will have professional and operational independence, particularly in matters in which their duties and responsibilities are categorically specified in law with little or no discretion and at the same time their overall performance can be effectively monitored and kept within the framework of the law by an agency which will involve the Government also.

B. Ideal Relationship between the Police and Government

The National Police Commission observed that in the existing set-up the (state) Government seek to have full control over the police by virtue of Section 3 of the Police Act 1861 – which is nearly 150 years old, enacted by an alien ruler, when the role and context of the police were vastly different. While evolving ideas regarding the nature of the relationship between the Government and the police, keeping in view demands of public interest and democratic polity, the NPC relied upon rulings of the Supreme Court of India, and laid down that "the power of superintendence of the State Government over the police should be limited for the purpose of ensuring that police performance is in strict accordance with law". In the context of public interest litigation, the Supreme Court has directed the State Governments to set up State Commissions, without any options to the state. In fact, it has set up rigid deadlines for action in this direction.

Broadly dividing the tasks of the police into three categories viz., (i) investigative; (ii) preventive; and (iii) service oriented, the NPC observed that as far as investigative tasks are concerned the nature of action to be taken on conclusion of investigation is a matter to be decided by the police only and by no other authority. It was reiterated that the investigative tasks of the police are beyond any kind of intervention by the political or police executive. Investigation is a professional, specialized task that brooks no dilution.

The NPC recognized that in the performance of 'preventive' tasks and 'service'–oriented functions (such as an industrial strike, communal tensions, etc.); the police will need to interact with other governmental agencies and service organizations. Thus, it has recommended that in the performance of preventive tasks and service-oriented functions, the police should be subject to the overall guidance from the government which should lay down broad policies for adoption in different situations from time to time.

C. Tenure and Appointment of the Chief of Police

Taking note of the weakening of the chain of command resulting from unauthorized interference with police work by political and other extraneous sources, and in order to restore the capacity of the police as an organization to resist such pressures and illegal or irregular orders, the NPC recommended that the chief of police in a state is assured of a statutory tenure of office without the Democles' sword of transfer hanging over his head all the time, subject to political whim. The NPC, while recommending a four-year term, hoped that such a tenure will strengthen his/her position and enable him to stand up effectively against pressures on the system. The massive transfers of police officers that has become almost the first ritual of most of the Chief Ministers soon after the swearing-in, testifies to the malice. The NPC has also recommended a fairly detailed procedure to ensure a proper selection of the person so that the selection is not put to abuse.

D. State Security Commission

Recognizing the scope for regulating the power of superintendence of the State Governments over the police, the NPC emphasized the immediate need to devise a new mechanism, christened the State Security Commission which would help the State Governments to discharge superintending responsibility in an open manner, under the framework of the law, with due regard to healthy norms and conventions in the course of time.

The Commission outlined the functions of the State Security Commission as to include:

(i) laying down broad policy guidelines and direction for the performance of preventive tasks and service-oriented functions by the police;
(ii) evaluation of the performance of the State Police every year and presenting a report to the respective State Legislatures;
(iii) functioning as a forum of appeal for disposing of representations from any police officer of the rank of Superintendent of Police and above regarding his being subjected to illegal or irregular orders in the performance of his duties;
(iv) functioning as a forum of appeal for disposing of representations from police officers regarding promotion of the rank of Superintendent of Police and above; and
(v) generally keeping in view the functioning of the police in the State.

The State Security Commissions, with statutory status, will have the respective State Minister in charge of police as the ex-officio Chairman and six other members, with the chief of police as ex-officio secretary of this Commission. Two of the six members shall be chosen from the legislature (one from the ruling party and another from the opposition parties) on the advice of the Speaker. Four members of the Commission shall be appointed by the Chief Minister, subject to approval by the State legislature, from among retired judges, retired Government servants, social scientists or academicians of public standing and eminence.

The NPC also recommended that the arrangements of funds for the functioning of this Commission will be made on the same lines as for the State Public Service Commission. The term of Members of the Commission shall be three years, which shall meet at least once every month.

E. Policy Direction or Guidelines

The NPC envisaged that as the Chairman of the Commission, the Minister-in-charge of police will be able to project the government point of view during the Commission's deliberations. Any policy direction or guidelines which the government desires to issue shall have to be agreed upon by the Commission before they are passed onto the police for implementation. It is also envisaged that, in an "emergency", the government may directly issue a policy direction or guidelines in regard to a specific situation, but such direction or guidelines shall, as soon as possible, be brought before the Commission for ratification and be subject to such modifications as the Commission might decide.

The National Police Commission hoped that the constitution of the state security commissions will help considerably in making police performance politically neutral, and that such responsibility is discharged in an open manner, while retaining governmental responsibility for overseeing the police.

F. Increasing Relevance in the Emerging Socio-Political Scenario

In the emerging socio-political scenario, as expressed in the widely-held clichés, such as politicization of crime, and criminalization of politics, the rationale for state-level Security Commissions emerges not merely from the need to protect police administration from political interference, but equality, if not more, to protect the democratic processes and the political system from the ineffectiveness and a wide variety of misdemeanours of the police. Since India became a Republic, many State Governments were dismissed more times on account of 'failure' of 'law and order', than perhaps all other counts put together. Thus, there is a vital public as much as political interest in promoting and sustaining autonomy and accountability of the police.

The increasing relevance for State (level) Security Commissions also arises from the fact that all political parties have blamed the 'party-in-power' of misuse and abuse of the police, as an instrument of the party (in power) rather than as an instrument of the state, accountable to law. All political parties have been in power, one time or the other, in some State or the other, and all political parties vouch for this shortcoming. Quantitative growth in the number of police forces, and sophisticated weaponry do not make for a professional and effective police force. The police leadership gives an impression of making feeble attempts at professionalization of the police, more perhaps on account of having to face internal pressures from the cadres. A measure of demoralization at the higher levels and frustration at the lower levels of the police organizations is being reflected in the conduct of and discipline at the cutting edge of police, destroying the image and credibility of police organizations in India.

The Indian police did contribute wards, with all the internal contradictions, limitations, and partisan political pressures, towards keeping our Republic intact. The Republic and the public have a legitimate interest in promoting autonomy, accountability and professionalism among the police forces through the setting up of the State Police Commissions in all the States of India. Such an institution can better address isolated issues such as privatization or outsourcing in a more comprehensive and professional manner. It is time for the political parties to get concerned about the vital issues of polity and act consensually.

Professionalization

Three sets of attributes emerge for consideration with reference to individual professionals, and professional organizations. They are: (a) specialized knowledge, (b) acquisition of skills in order to be able to apply such knowledge on the job, in real-life situations, and (c) a set of socially acceptable value premises and an ethical framework; these attributes characterize all the professions. Acquisition of specialized knowledge, including updation and upgradation through continuing education in a formal or informal setting, and the techniques and skills required to be able to use such knowledge. Induction, apprenticeship and on-the-job training are some of the other modes of imparting or acquiring skills in order to be able to deliver competent service, efficiently. But, it is the third attribute viz., value premises and an ethical framework that represent a critical variable for it is this attribute that characterizes the utilization of human resources in the form of excellence in professional performance. Access to professional services, at an affordable cost, a positive role in shaping the social agenda, and translating such agenda, operating within a code of ethics, self-regulation (in disciplining deviant and errant members of the profession) social accountability of professional/ organizational performance, insulating members of the profession from the ills operating within the society, are some of the important, socially acceptable value premises and ethical standards of all professions. Professions acquire, sustain and enhance their professional status and image through a process of legitimization, and a periodic articulation of and commitment to the attributes of professionalism. These attributes can be contextualized and concretized with reference to the respective professions such as teaching, medicine, journalism, management and public administration. That police personnel and police organizations constitute a profession cannot be over emphasized. While all other professions have their own respective codes of ethics to be subscribed and conformed to by the members at the time of their entry into the profession, the police is the only one to have three codes of professional conduct in India: one formulated by the police themselves (1960), the second, set out by the Government of India

(MHA, 1985), and the third by the United Nations, for all the law enforcing organizations all over the world 1979.

Professionalism contributes not only to the credibility of an organization, but also to the efficacy of its role as an agent of social transformation. Contrarily, dilution of professional ethics, on the part of an individual or an organization not only leads to societal condemnation and internal demoralization, but also social turbulence, and distortions in the process of social transformation. The attributes of 'professionalism' vis-à-vis self-centred 'careerism' as well as the implications of the two alternatives are profiled in Illustration 13.

The adversaries of police forces are growing tech-savvy rapidly, having an effective network of arms-*bazaars,* abroad as well as within the country. They have an easy access to these *bazaars*. The adversaries have equipped themselves with a wide range of high-tech tools such as mobile telephones, internet, high-frequency wireless communication, etc., and access to technical expertise so much so that they often outsmart the security forces. They have wireless repeater stations deep in the jungles which provide a multiplier effect. They can intercept the wireless communications of the police organizations. The reach of their communication network is global; they use encryption software.

The Peoples War (PW) claims that it has a deadly arsenal.[47] Besides organizational skills, matching or sometimes excelling the police organizations, P.W. has acquired the skills of manufacturing arms. Arms experts estimate and depict a comparison of arms between the police and 'Peoples' War in Andhra Pradesh State as in Illustration 14.

The police forces also have to reckon with the 'non-state actors' creating conditions of nuclear, chemical and biological warfare. The smallest amount of plutonium, about the size of an apple, could kill and injure hundreds of thousands of innocent people. Terrorist networks such as Al-Qaeda have tried to acquire the material for improvising a nuclear weapon. This situation had warranted the Nuclear Security Summit (Washington Apr. 2010) attracting delegates from 50 countries, with nearly half of them heads of nations and/or of governments, to take note of the reality

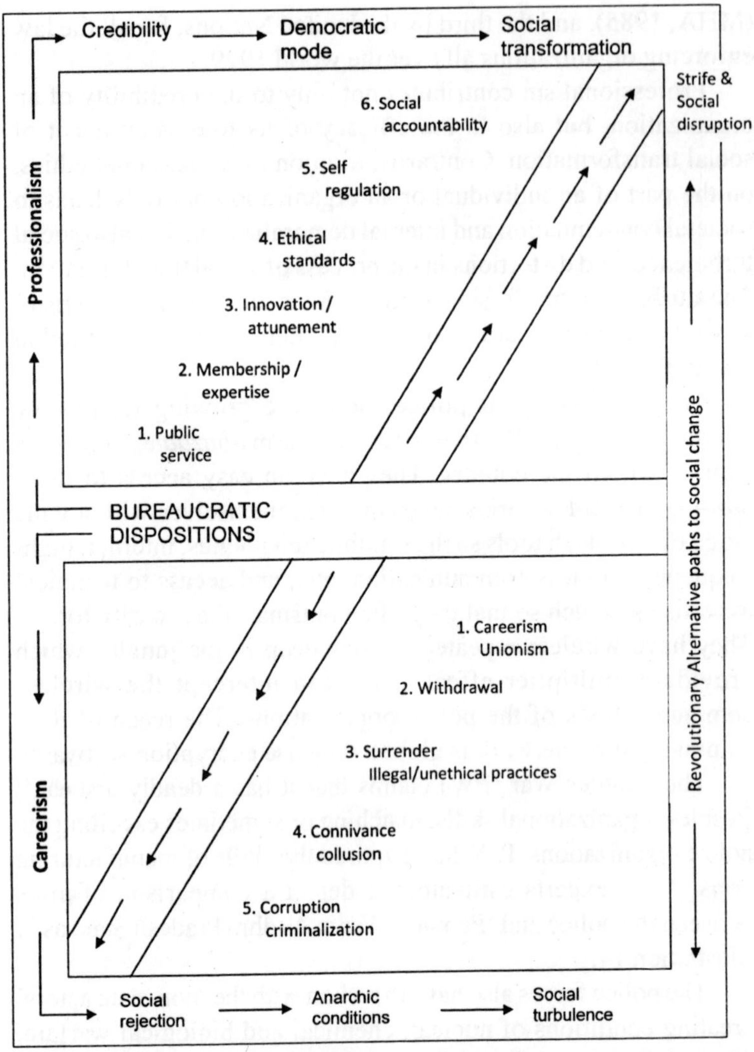

Illustration 13: Attributes of Professionalism: Alternatives and Implications

of technological advances registered by the anti-democratic forces. As a military expert has observed recently, the security forces have to play the game of national security with those who have a technological edge to win the war. In the contemporary context,

Sl. No.	AP Police	Peoples' War
1	Rifles : .303	Rifles : .303
2	Self Loading Rifles (SLR) : AK 47	Self Loading Rifles (SLR) : AK 45
3	Light Machine Gun (LMG)	Light Machine Gun (LMG) 9 mm Carbine
4	Medium Machine Gun (MMG) 9 mm Carbine	
5	Short Weapons : Revolver 9 mm pistol, Glock pistol	Short Weapons : Revolver, pistol, Crude weapons (Tapancha)
		Guns : 12 bore guns manufactured by the PW Tech Unit
6	Launchers : Grenade launcher; Tear Gas shell launcher, 2 mm Mortars	Launchers : Successfully test fired motor manufactured by its members
7	Explosives : Hand grenades. Improvised Explosive Devises	Explosives : Hand grenades, Land mines made with gelatin, Claymore Mines Timer devices triggered by camera flash
8	Communication equipment High frequency wireless network, Cellular phones. Satellite phones underway.	Communication equipment want of internet OTG Cellular phones.
9	Other gadgets : Dragon lights, night vision goggles, jungle boots. A helicopter for use in times of emergency	Other gadgets : Ordinary torch lights and ordinary footwear. Do not use vehicles as they move in jungles.

Illustration 14: Range of Arms and Equipment – Andhra Pradesh Police and Peoples War Group (PWG): A Comparative Profile

we need a highly knowledgeable, skilled and positively motivated police force, not just a 'lathi-force'; or 'trigger-happy' police of the yester-decades. In India we are adding numbers faster than modernization and trying to spread the technology thin with potentially dire consequences to the police as much as to the nation. In order to become both efficient and effective a police force, needs to promote both modernization and professionalism.

The Indian polity has not yet been able to overcome the decisional conflict, over what type of legal framework is needed to fight anti-democratic forces so as to be able to protect our democratic fabric. The police continues to be misused, abused and stands demoralized. The police have to learn to save themselves, so as to succeed in saving India's democracy. There are so many democratic countries in the comity of nations who have acted in right earnest, with visible and measurable results. India gives the impression that it has placed the issues on the national agenda, but is waiting for the daybreak. India is stuck with a legal framework devised for the 19th century. The police is not exempt from the malignancy of a partisan political process. The Union Home Ministry is still engaged in a debate over VIP security.

There is an enormous, ever-mounting number of policemen who are giving their life in order to protect the democratic fabric of the nation. In all solemnity, the 'Police Commemoration Day' is observed ritualistically on the 21st October every year, by the police organizations. Should the nation not join, in reverence, the Commemoration Day events? And should not the nation aim at zero-fatalities on the part of police forces? There is a deplorable hiatus between the people and the police – it's growing, with no attempts visible anywhere to bridge the gulf.

What can and should the police do where the polity is divided, fragmented, and fractured by ideological, separatist, insurgent, religious, pan— Islamic groups, or, sheer criminal gangs committing heinous crimes on minor girls? These and many more similar crises, nay, flash points of democracy, the police have to answer for themselves and to the polity. They can't wait or afford to ignore, for they have a mission to fulfill, uphold the majesty of 'rule of law' and sustain their ultimate accountability to society.

The police on its part, in spite of an internal debate (annual police science congress, annual meet of DGs, re-union meets, professional police associations, and apex professional organizations like BPR&D, SVPNPA, and the ISA have not adequately helped themselves to contain the erosion of the image of the police in society. Are the police organizations and their leaders showing signs of isolation, withdrawal, institutional enervation and atrophy? The challenge is to restore public understanding, cooperation and support without endangering the accomplishment of a delicate, difficult and 'unpopular' mission. Indeed, society recognizes the critical role of the police, and believes in its capabilities. The society keeps assigning more and more delicate tasks, and budgetary allocations to the police. Can the police take on all the increasing demands and meet the expectations of society, without resolving their own dilemmas, and improving their performance? Instead of squarely facing such a set of dilemmas, the reflections often heard in India today are such as: "A society gets the police it deserves", and that "police is also a part of the society", and hence they reflect all the ills prevailing in society"! Such dispositions smack of a loss of the professional character, and a dilution of the resolve to restore its professional role, image and credibility. The police are neither able to implement public policy as formulated, nor able to say effectively that they cannot implement the policy as formulated. Can the police implement a policy in the shaping of which they have had no role? Do the police organizations and their leadership represent a case of withdrawal from their professional role and responsibility in shaping public policy in regard to the way policing is done and national security managed?

A society is involved in the process of rapid social change, but the police organizations have remained relatively static. The objectives of the police and their role in society have, and continue to undergo change, but the organizations have not changed – structure, culture, systems and attitudes – in tune with the changing objectives. Police organizations are growing larger, and increasingly being centralized, devoid of participative processes within and without. Society is seeking to move away from casteism, communalism, and sectarianism; the police are tending to show partisan bias, even if selectively, leading to society making demands such as 'minority' police and 'tribal battalions'.

Using the subterfuge of accountability to the people, the

politicians outside have come to acquire a complete stranglehold over the police. Police leadership is neither protesting nor showing signs that they have the will to protect over their organizational image. Police today act without their own independent will, perhaps against their own conscience. The morale of the force has suffered a serious erosion due to antiquated laws, uncooperative public, an alert and activist press, constantly interfering politicians, multiplicity of command, unattractive working conditions, self-centred leadership, and a variety of similar factors. When the organization does not provide institutional mechanisms for resolving dilemmas, and aberrations such as encounter deaths, blinding, and other modes of police violence occur leaders with professional ethos feel suffocated, and observe in moments of unguarded introspection, making statements such as "it is better to disband the I.P.S." India's democratic polity certainly needs the IPS, the demos feel.

Police in India have to operate, like every other organization, within the framework of the law and in conformity with the Indian Constitution. The police have been placed on a higher pedestal by society and assigned greater responsibility in preserving and promoting the rule of law. That is why the actions of the police are constantly scrutinized by the judiciary, legislature and by the people at large. The popular image is that often police actions are arbitrary, sans accountability.

In a recent survey, it was revealed that a majority of the police officers desire absolute accountability to law, and to the government, and thus to the community. Police officers all over India agree that the prevailing 'accountability' tends to be to the local political functionary, the Home Minister, and often directly to the chief minister of the state. This control by the political functionaries tends to dilute the accountability of the police to law and to the society. Police officers are conscious of the fact that this politicization, collusion and corruption are responsible for the present state of the negative image of the police in India. The recommendation of the National Police Commission (1978), for the setting up of a state-level State Security Commission as a buffer between the political bosses and police organizations, acquires primacy. It is in the context of the increasing criticality of the role of the police in upholding and sustaining the democratic order of society, and in facilitating and promoting social transformation that constitutes the challenge before the Indian republic and the professionalization of the police assumes critical significance, the *sine qua non*.

Today, we have a large network of training institutions that help update knowledge, and upgradation of skills, as an integral part of 'modernization' of the forces. It is disheartening to note the very low levels of awareness even among officers, of the existence of codes of conduct and ethics for the police. Codes of ethics are neither to be preserved in the archives, nor for mere decoration of the walls. The codes have to flow through the length and breadth of police organizations, like electrical energy that electrifies. Such conformity has to be made known to the public as well. The codes encompass *Swadharma* – individual conduct, as much as *Samsthagat* and *Samajik dharma*, of the collective. Police training and development have to be fine tuned, and energized in order to electrify all levels of the organization. It is not utopian, for today, such committed leadership is available, at different levels, within the police organizations.

All professions strive to attain excellence, on a continuing basis. It is for the police leadership to formulate standards of excellence, measure the levels of excellence attained, and report to the society in order to seek and secure support and recognition. Towards this end, issues of professionalism can be formulated for an empirical examination and analysis:

- What are the "value dispositions" of police personnel as agents of change in the process of democratic development?
- How do they recognize the distortions of democratic development, and resolve their own dilemmas in making police organizations both effective and efficient?
- What are the attributes of professionalism and the implications (to the society and to the police) emerging from their increasing or declining degrees of professionalism?

- How do the police comply with the ethical standards that they have set for themselves and meet the problems of self-regulation in the face of pressures from the society.
- Finally, how far do the police recognize and seek to fulfill their social accountability?

Today, the society, (as much as the police leadership) is concerned about 'policing the police', demanding adequate and appropriate institutional mechanisms and processes. All professional groups have society as their reference point for their professional status. It is only when the police prove their credibility and accountability to the society will society lend support to the police. The equations between the community and the police have to be built on the firm foundations of social accountability, leading to mutual support.

Policing the police is going out of hand of the leadership of police organizations, in several directions. The purpose is best served by initiating the process of 'social audit', in collaboration with the society. Social audit does not mean loss of initiative for the police. Police can also undertake a periodical exercise of the nature and manner of problems tackled, and the problems encountered by the police in serving the society. Social audit promotes transparency and also secures support from the community. There are many instances where police officers have successfully utilized public opinion as a powerful force to counter partisan political pressures.

Professional standards are not static or fixed, but are constantly fine tuned to the process of social evolution, though they essentially revolve round standards of service to the society, and with a focus on excellence in performance. Of equal importance, are the processual dimensions of self-regulation protecting and preserving the autonomous character provided by society. The normative and the processual dimensions of professionalization enhance, in the ultimate analysis, the process of legitimization, social acceptability, image, credibility, job satisfaction and self-esteem.

The Supreme Court verdict restricting the use of narco-analysis and similar techniques on suspects is welcomed by some sections of people, while others maintain that the ruling is a setback to scientific investigation. A demand is growing in volume that the parliament may provide for a statutory base to permit polygraph and brain-mapping tests. As stated by some eminent jurists, the law runs parallel to life. The material conditions of life have changed in the era of extremists and terrorists, *Swadeshi* or *Videshi*. A person like Kasab, caught on CCTV, and apprehended before the eyes of hundreds of witnesses, he who had confessed to the crime (of waging war against India) takes cool advantage of Article 20(3) of the Constitution which embodies the guarantee against self-incrimination ('no person accused of an offence shall be compelled to be a witness against himself'). Law enforcing and justice dispensing functionaries together have to find a solution to deal with those 'enemies' of the nation adopting anti-democratic violent and extremist acts of violence against India, its citizens, and their democratic way of life.

Police organizations and their leadership have to don their thinking caps, with regard to issues such as third-degree methods, encounter deaths, torture, coercion, etc. It is admitted by the police and even army leaders like David Perry of the US Army War College, who rightly observe that "the available interrogation options may all be bad in some way". Similarly, on some other issues of security management, there has not emerged a point of clarity, a clear line of thinking. The centre-state equations and role-relationships continue to swing like a pendulum. It seems to be that we have not come out of the yester-year contentious dialogue of federalism and a strong-centre vis-à-vis strong state, whereas the people want a strong nation. Have the police any option? If so, what is their professionally preferred option? At least they should debate within their own organizations, and then engage the polity.

The implications of democratization for police organizations are two fold – to adjust and attune the organization to the political transition, and secondly, organizational reengineering, in terms of cooptation with Panchayati Raj Institutions (PRIs). The police cannot swim, for long, against the mainstream of democratization. And police cannot, and shall not take distorted policy decisions, as 'given' by partisan political processes. Police have a professional role and responsibility, to help shape the policy process by providing 'professional' inputs on the one hand and promoting awareness among the public in order to facilitate informed democratic discourse on the other. If policing is too complex to be left to the play of partisan politics, it cannot be left to the police either, in exclusive terms.

Police may have been a 'disciplined' and a highly skilled 'specialist' organization. But, it has not been a thinking, much less an 'interacting' organization so as to get a mirror image of itself.

A professionalized police organization would, illustratively, a) seek to influence and shape public policy rather than take policy as 'given', (b) cannot act passively and then adopt a posture of helplessness. "What can we do?", (c) lend clarity to issues such as secularism and 'Naxalism' rather than get choked by the shifting policies based on distorted political processes, (d) condemn unprofessional practices such as 'third-degree methods', deficient if not faulty investigations, contrived evidence and encounters which lead to judicial strictures and public condemnation, (e) function as promoters of the rule of law, protectors of human rights (it is only when police are found inadequate or partisan that victims go to remedial institutions such as Human Rights Commissions or to the judicial institutions); and (f) establish positive, live, reciprocal communication with the public in educating them about the rule of law, and the role of the citizen in promoting the same as partners in a democratic polity.

The role of the police has changed significantly, but the changes, which occurred hitherto pale into insignificance compared to the emerging challenges. Are the police organizations preparing today in order to be able to take on the emerging demands of society? For e.g. it is now recognized that social harmony is a prerequisite as well as an integral part of social transformation, and that the police as a peace force would play a role in the promotion of social harmony and resolution of social conflict.

A police officer analyzed the criminal justice policy (or the lack of it) and identified a variety of factors in the law, in the system and in the society which are responsible for the increasing criminality and the decreasing efficiency of the police in controlling it. Pointing out the lack of a dynamic and coordinated policy in the face of accelerated social change, he observed that, "Even under the most favourable circumstances, the capacity of the police to act against crime is limited. The police do not create and cannot resolve the socio-economic conditions that activate crime. They are not responsible for the convulsions arising out of cultural pluralism. They do not foment labour agitation, nor do they resort to *Gherao* and *Bandh*. The police do not set the students on the rampage. They struggle to function as an oasis in a desert of indiscipline which is an endemic disease in our society. They are expected to be different from the general matrix of the society to which they belong. They do not enact the laws which they are required to enforce. They are not expected to sit in judgment over the criminals whom they arrest. Crime which is a social phenomena has to be tackled by society. If increasing crime has to be effectively dealt with, a holistic approach on the part of society is essential. Such a holistic picture emerges only when police participate in public policy. Society cannot stand by the police, unless police stands by the society. Once police go to the aid of the society, society supports the police. This mutuality is facilitated and promoted by the ethos of decentralization, participation, and professionalization."[47]

The design of police organizations in India represents a fine example of *de jure* decentralization, with the Station House Officer/s legally vested with the responsibility and matching authority for accountable performance. But the reality on the ground is that the SHO is ineffective and dysfunctional because *de facto,* his/her initiative and authority are wrested by higher levels and an ever-increasing layers, who are far removed from the point of action. It may be more realistic, perhaps, to state that the authority is divorced from responsibility and vice versa. It is not even centralized at the top, but slips out of the police organization. The cutting edge level of police i.e. the SHO, becomes the butt of popular ridicule; the cutting edge gets blunted.

In any 'organization', the logic of division of labour is such that the top tier concerns itself with policy, the middle tiers with coordination, and the bottom rung with operations. Where the top gets involved in the operations, it makes the other two tiers ineffective. As the top itself cannot do justice to its own task of taking an effective role in the policy process, and securing policy support from the polity, they fail the organizations, of which the middle as well as the operational levels get fully aware of, and get affected adversely along with the public in general.

With increasing degrees of centralization, *espirit de crops*, the elixir of organizations, gets extinct, and the participative culture dries up, with disastrous consequences of decreasing morale, motivation and efficacy. Alienation takes the place of participation. Participative processes within an organization can be likened to the circulation of blood in a human body, cleansing and life-sustaining. Devoid of participative ethos and culture, organizations suffer from blood clots. The participative process facilitates cascading of the structure, and jelling of roles. Devoid of that sense of involvement, the law of nature, characterized by the instinct of survival takes over, leading to a situation where all the levels establish, or seek to establish, extraneous (political, criminal or other) linkages, leading to organizational short circuits.

Trade unionism initiated at the level of constabulary can spread, in its myriad forms, to the middle tiers of police organizations. It might spread even to the senior levels of the organization. Any debate on reform and rejuvenation of the police often leads to the argument around 'system' versus 'man', and an equation with 'chick or egg first'. It is a trite saying that systems can only be as good as the people who operate and 'man' the system. Leadership is an ability to say "give me any system, I shall make it work". Policemen are citizens too, in the first place. Let them not distance themselves, much less the police organization, from the society. Let them participate actively in the democratic process, and strengthen it, in the process strengthening the positive equations between society and the police.[49]

Can the police explore and derive the strength of a positive democratic process by organizing a 'Citizens Committee' not of the partisan model, at the level of each Station House, at least experimentally, and informally to start with? There are proximate examples and successful experiments in this direction. This grass-roots democratization could strengthen the SHO. Further, it can counter initially, but negate in the long-term, malignant or partisan politicization that creeps in from outside. Such a process calls for a) openness of the police organization, and b) a change in the orientation of the police from 'power' and 'authority' to one of 'transparency' and 'accountability'. The police need not wait for society to demand this democratization. They can initiate the process on their own. Unfortunately, available evidence suggests that the police had resisted such cooptation with the Panchayati Raj Institutions on grounds that such cooptation will dilute their role, power and authority. They insisted and succeeded in reversing a legislated norm in this regard, in the state of Karnataka. The National Police Commission has strongly recommended the setting up, at the state level of a state security commission. The political parties, including the Janata Party, during whose regime the Commission was set up, did not show great interest in acting on the recommendations. But what is the disposition of the police organizations towards this significant proposal which would have matched autonomy for the police with accountability and the responsibility of the police, minimizing at the same time the malignant influence of the political process? The Indian polity did not have the benefit of the views of the police in this direction. Perhaps their silence speaks more eloquently. The citizens had actually campaigned for and supported the proposal. Indeed, the credibility of public institutions was the leading issue during the 1989 elections. It is high time for the police to move in the direction of autonomy matching with accountability, and take the organization nearer the people, and to that extent, away from partisan politicization.

The police has made a breakthrough in establishing a correlation between autonomy and accountability in the form of commissionerates for cities. With the villages, called the sleeping giants thus far, waking up, the need for rural policing has become urgent. Can the police take on the new task, with their existing limitations? Does it not represent a case for organizational innovations?

A churning process could also result in a restatement of the role of the police which got blurred over a period of time. A law and order organization by statutory definition has taken upon itself, or has been loaded with, without protest, such a wide range of unrelated tasks, compromising and diluting its primary role. It takes a long time to restore its identity, role, image and efficacy. It would be relevant to ask: How come such a wide variety of tasks, unrelated to their role, which they are ill equipped to perform, have been dumped on the police without as much as a protest? And what is the way out, if there is any?

Democratization of the police both internally and externally will help police organizations and the society to redefine the role of the police. Such a redefinition, *de novo*, could lead to offloading the avalanche of social legislation of which neither the legislature nor the police have been able to keep track of. The police have to re-establish their equations with, and their role in the society afresh, through a creative exploration and interaction. Whatever may be the specifics, one strategy that the police have to explore is to take the people on their side. Without taking active support, cooperation and involvement of the people, call it democratization or whatever, the police can never be a success. But in the case of the police, at this juncture such a strategy is impeded perhaps by the fact that they are not on 'talking' terms with the demos, the people in our democracy. So, the tumbler of mutual prejudices has to be emptied first before it is filled with positive dispositions and attitudes.

Issues of professionalism among police personnel and their organizations in India emerge in the context of constitutional democracy. Democratic governance and social transformation generate certain dilemmas and conflicts within the police organizations and among their leadership, exposing them to several and severe stresses and strains. Professional ethics provide a way out of the dilemmas and conflicts and help the police perform their role effectively and efficiently. Modernization (which encompasses facets such as upgradation of techniques and technologies of detection and investigation of crime, and punishment; computerization, introduction of sophisticated arms and ammunition and communication technology), contribute to but do not, *per se* represent professionalization of the police and their organizations. Professionalism represents the qualitative dimension of an organization in the service of the community. It represents the value-orientations of people, and reflects the ethos of an organization enhancing its credibility, esteem and image. Devoid of such an ethos, any organization will lose its credibility, which leads to social rejection, to varying degrees. Leadership constitutes a critical variable in enhancing the levels of professionalism in any organization.

5

Challenge of Change: Strategic Initiatives

Managing Change

It is axiomatic that 'change' is the only 'constant' in human society. Consequently, social institutions created by humans, be it a family, a corporate organization or an institution of state, have to take cognizance of social change and attune and adjust themselves, constantly, to the process of change in society. A series of issues emerge, especially before the leadership of organizations. Some of the important questions are: (1) What are the elements of social change? What are their dimensions and dynamics? (2) What is the nature of interaction between the society, its process of change, and organizations, which operate within the society? Is that influence unidirectional or reciprocal? (3) What could be the framework for the analysis and appraisal of organizations – their performance and measurement of productivity? Under the conditions of change, and (4) what are the parameters for the modus of management of organizational change? These and many more similar issues bring to the fore a set of conceptual and ideological facets which help shape strategies of management to cope with change. Briefly, these issues can be focused on the police organizations in India, in an illustrative framework. A detailed, empirical and analytical exercise with reference to any specific police organization, such as the CRPF, or a, civilian police organization in any state, would be fascinating and insightful.

Change takes place in a variety of ways, at all times, though the pace may vary; and change can be seen from many an angle.

Broadly, the process of change can be seen in terms of three clusters, viz., (a) values, value-sets shaping ideological dispositions and premises, (b) socio-economic conditions, and (c) technological factors. The change process forms a continuum, of the past, the present, and futuristic directions. Both the 'evolutionary' and 'revolutionary' dynamics of change fit into this continuum. An overview of the interface between the factors and dynamics of social change is presented in Illustration 15.

It is the futuristic aspirations, ideals and vision of the people in any society, that operate as the beacon light for organizational change management. In no society and at no point of time are the diverse factors of change in fusion with each other, nor do they contribute to change at the same pace. There is a constant inter-play and society remains, always in a state of flux. That is why, at any given point of time, there is a wide variation between different societies, as well as between groups within any society. This is how the factors of change generate and represent a maze of competing and conflicting values, interests and identities. It is the function of the political process in society, and the leadership of organizations, to harmonize these competing and conflicting factors with reference to the long-term ideals and vision of that society. This process can be illustrated with reference to (a) the freedom movement leading to democratization (with emphasis on liberty and freedom); (b) the Indian Constitution promising the translation of human rights (political, economic social and cultural) into a reality; individualism of a liberal society and atomization of joint families into nuclear families; globalization and liberalization of economies; information technology triggering 'revolutionary' changes in communication, and operation of divergently opposite processes such as centralization of authority and decentralization of organization structures. Such processes can be enumerated endlessly.

It is the society that creates and sustains organizations, it also generates pressure on organizations to change. Society also discards the extant, and also innovates new organizations in order to subserve its dynamic needs. Thus, organizations have to constantly (a) monitor the process of social change, (b) cope with the emerging

1.0 SOCIAL CHANGE		
Process of change →	**Past Present Future →**	**Continuum →**
Factors of change 1. Ideological 2. Socio-economic 3. Technological	Situation Reality Vision Competing / Conflicting 1. Values 2. Interests 3. Identities	Vision, Ideals Social Transformation

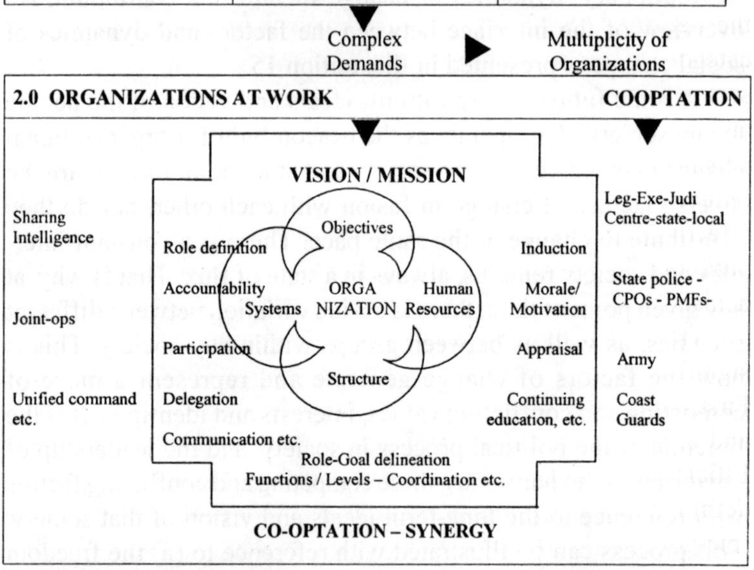

3.0 DYNAMIC MODE			
REDEFINE	REDESIGN	MONITOR	APPRAISE
Refine objectives prioritize set performance - standards SWOT	Role-Goal clarity Coordination Cooptation Design / Induct Management Information Systems	Customer/citizen satisfaction Quality of service Cost Modernization	Productivity, Espirit de corps, Training needs Analysis, Change modes

4.0 TOWARDS EXCELLENCE : INTEGRATE TRG. RES. ORG. DEV.		
• Scan / Forecast environment • Monitor Social Change • Mark policy issues • Evaluation of performance	• Attune values / attitudes upgrade knowledge / skills • Formulate agenda and strategies for change Develop internal change agents	• Professionalization, Negotiate / shape inputs. Secure external inputs; Protect from external pollutants; Initiate action for change

Illustration 15: Managing Change in Police Organizations

and changing trends and demands (c) harmonize the competing and conflicting demands, into organizational objectives; and (d) prepare the organization to contribute to such objectives. The more efficient organizations do not wait for the society to make fresh demands in tune with the social change. They keep a constant watch over emerging change, innovate and prepare in advance to meet the demands in a more 'proactive' manner. There is also the category of organizations (especially in the competitive corporate sector) that generate conditions (in the manner of needs) of change and convert them into markets for profits. The lag between fresh demands from the society and organizational response has to be reduced, if not eliminated. There are organizations, which are effective but are not efficient and vice-versa. Performance and productivity depend upon both external effectiveness meeting the demands, and internal efficiency (mode of meeting the demands).

Three responses on the part of organizations assume critical significance in the management of their interface with the society. First, the society – almost all the societies and at all times – generate and assign contradictory, competing and conflicting demands. Efficient organizations facilitate and help themselves with a precise definition of their role so as to reduce demand-response gap, and role-goal conflict. It is a function of the organizational leadership. Emerging from the logic of the first, no professional organization takes 'policy' as 'given' but assumes an active role in 'shaping' policy so as to ensure role-goal clarity without ambiguity or conflict. The degree of role clarity and image of organizational leadership are directly correlated. All organizations contribute to the shaping of the future vision of the society of which they are a part, and spontaneously contribute towards the fulfillment of such a vision. Futurological explorations, mapping out a vision of the future, and translation of such a vision into a reality represent the most creative opportunity and a constant challenge to any organization. It is such an understanding that helps in shaping the organizational responses, promoting an image of creativity.

Organizational responses to the constant process of social change, and societal demands may be seen as falling into four facets labeled as: (a) clarity over the organizational objectives, (e.g. Protecting and promoting human rights); (b) re-structuring (fine tuning) the organization so as to be able to meet the changing needs and objectives (e.g. community policing); (c) designing and induction of support systems (e.g. performance appraisal) as management aids and finally, (d) the most critical one viz., human resources development and management (e.g. training needs analysis and, continuing education) also as a constant.

There is always a wide range of 'interest groups', and an equally wide-range of 'interests'. Harmonization of these wide range of competing and conflicting interests constitutes an integral part of formulation of the 'Mission' of any organization. At the level of a nation it is for the national leadership to formulate the national vision, by harmonizing divergent and occasionally conflicting interests. Similarly, it is for the organizational leaders to recognize the wide ranging expectations, and reconcile, harmonize and prioritize them. What is more, since no social environment remains stagnant but undergoes constant change, harmonizing divergent and conflicting interests is a 'constant' function of organizational leadership.

In order to ensure organizational effectiveness, on a continuing basis an 'environmental watch' or scan is essential to find out the changing 'futuristic' expectations and fine-tuning the organizational objectives. It is the responsibility of organizational leadership not only to respond, but to forecast 'futuristic' demands, negotiate with the society (polity), and prepare in good time, their organizations in order to meet those futuristic demands. Where this does not happen, organizations tend to loose their credibility and utility, leading to disuse, misuse and abuse, culminating into their 'demise', since society rejects them as non-performing and as irrelevant. Institutions are not only marginalized and rejected, societies also indulge in 'mercy-killing' of organizations that are out-of-tune with the changing times. Practices such as earlier 'nationalization' (1950-75) and contemporary privatization (1975-2000), disinvestment, etc. may reflect the 'whimsical' changes in societies. Talk of privatization or outsourcing of some aspects of policing represents a glaring example. Measures, like the Social safety net, golden handshake, and the like represent the palliatives to make mercy killing less painful. Society adopts diverse modes in either marginalizing or appreciating the 'net worth' of an organization, by creating collateral institutions to operate in a parallel, complementary or hierarchial manner, with the pre-existing ones. The rising image of the Central Bureau of Investigation (CBI) since its inception, downward slide in its credibility later on, leading to the emergence of the National Investigation Agency (NIA) dramatically demonstrate it in the sphere of police organizations.

The enormous range of policing organizations obtaining today reflects a maze of parallel, complementary, as well as competing and conflicting equations. The central police organizations, and adjunct investigative and intelligence organizations best illustrate these 'parallels'. The federal equations, and the legislative-executive-judicial complementary institutions in relation to the role of the police constitute the network of institutions. Such a network of institutions may have complementary tasks but common objectives. They have to work in unison, in a collaborative manner, but in the reality of organizations at work, they tend to generate conflicting perceptions of role as well as that of goal hierarchies. The functional complementarity and commonality of objectives warrant co-optation especially in aspects such as, intelligence sharing, joint deployment and a unified command. Under the conditions obtaining on the ground, several extraneous factors, such as: (a) a high degree of partisan-politicization of the police forces, (b) fear of deployment of the central police forces as amounting to central 'intervention' under Article 356 of the Constitution, (c) different political parties and leadership running the government in states expressing loss of confidence in the efficacy and neutrality of the state police, (d) a changing and growing tendency to demand central police, para-military and even armed forces in managing internal security, natural calamities and disaster situations. Absence of complementarity is best illustrated, in its most dysfunctional manifestation, between the magistracy and the police in regard to bail, and between some of the state police and the CRPF units operating in extremist situations, where some state police personnel had adopted tactics to disprove the efficacy of the central forces. A change process percolates, has to percolate, among the complementary institutions; and between the various units and tiers within an organization, in a reciprocal manner, uniformly at all times. When some officers take the initiative establishing bridges between organizations and in managing organizational changes, transfer of officers without any rule or rhythm, negate such initiatives.

Where the society at large (at the level of communities, nations and on an universal basis) is dynamic, even to stay where they are, in terms of excellence in performance, organizations have to keep moving. Organizational management has to be dynamic in order to attain and maintain a level of excellence on a continuing basis. There are four processes that help organizations retain dynamism and promote excellence in performance. These can be identified as (a) **Redefine** role and objectives, (b) **Redesign** (reengineer) structure, and supporting systems, (c) **Monitor** citizen (consumer) orientations, and concerns for quality and cost, and (d) **Appraise** organizational performance regularly.

SWOT is an exercise in the analysis of internal strengths and weaknesses, as well as external opportunities and threats to any organization. SWOT exercise should be neither esoteric nor occasional but a meticulous and constant process, for it serves as a preventive check-up on the status of organizational health, rather than as a remedial treatment.

Redesigning (re-engineering) the organization, on a continuing basis in tune with the changing (expanding/contracting) role, objectives and performance standards set out is a necessity. Design changes would also encompass the processes of cooptation (joint operations, command and control) and various management support processes (such as decentralization as for e.g., creation of range Inspectors General or DIGs), community participation vis-à-vis *Panchayati Raj* Institutions (PRIs) and *Nyaya Panchayats*. Redesigning acquires significance in promoting role-goal clarity and congruence. Redefinition and Redesign integrate and harmonize the external changes and the consequential organizational change management.

Monitoring the citizen/consumer satisfaction and dissatisfaction along with time, quality and cost specifications constitute the third dimension of management for promoting excellence in performance. They provide the benchmark for measuring the degree and direction of either excellence or slippages in performance, warranting diverse corrective measures. Since police organizations have to cater to the society at large, stake-holder interactions help in setting standards and would help meet all the performance standards set, and in the formulation of plans for organizational development. It must be recognized that keeping citizens on their side secured a lot of strength to a large number of police officers at various levels. Such 'leaders' used public support to counterveil partisan pressures on police organizations.

Development of the Organization (OD) encompasses all the managerial modes and processes that would help remedy the shortfalls and shortcomings, as well as help in promoting excellence on a continuing basis. OD encompasses the management of human resources (Job descriptions, clarity, induction, enhancement of knowledge and skills, promotion of work ethic and organizational culture including discipline, training needs analyses in relation to changing roles and tasks; and performance appraisal). Of equal importance, if not more, is the induction and utilization of technological aids and modernization, as an integral part of the process of professionalization of police organizations. Excellence in performance is a function of and results from a holistic agenda for what may be called Training Research and Organization Development (TROD).

An integrated agenda of TROD for enhancing the external effectiveness, internal efficiencies and the management of change can be formulated methodically. A precise agenda, along with identification of priorities and strategies, can only be formulated on the basis of a detailed study of a specific organizational situation. Each project emerging either as a Training, Research, or Organization Development initiative has to be integrated, backward and forward, in holistic terms.

Five aspects of an organization emerge to be reckoned in any plan of action covering TROD. The process of change in the external world within which police need to manage themselves is 'caused' by the dynamics of society. Police organizations cannot stand-off in isolation, mutely, at the 'receiving end', but should also contribute positively to the cumulative process of social change. It is important for police organizations to enter into the realm of futurology in understanding the process, identifying the implications and exploring the modes of contributing to and shaping the process of change. During the times when factors such as democratization, revolution of human rights, liberalization and millennial development goals are sweeping the world, the police have to appreciate the significance of these processes, prepare themselves, in advance to fine-tune their mission. As the role of the police is changing in a swift and multifarious manner, such as the shift from managers of 'status quo' to that of managers at change, police seem to be standing on quicksand. The ground conditions are changing rapidly and radically. Police cannot be mute spectators. They have to be participants in the process of change. This calls for long-term planning, and constant reiteration and validation of their organizational mission.

The second aspect of the agenda may be towards quantification of the qualitative changes taking place. It is the statistical mode, not merely photo-static, but, also linear and comparative. This is proximate to, but not the same as the crime statistical series (being brought out by the National Crime Records Bureau NCRB). Just as qualitative data is quantified, quantitative data also needs qualitative analysis. It has to go beyond the analysis of trends. It should encompass the analytical mode so as to be able to arrive at cause and effect relationships and futuristic projections. A large number of research questions emerge from the valuable data documented by the NCRB. Answers and explanations to such questions will help the 'development' of police organizations.

The third aspect of agenda revolves round issues and concepts such as (a) secularism, naxalism, communalization of the police, (b) 'internal democracy'; implications of decentralized participative democracy (Panchayati Raj system), 'modelling' police organizations towards community policing, (c) 'nuances of the four-fold human rights', vis-à-vis implications for and the role of police, (d) implications and operational nuances of nuclear chemical and biological 'warfare'; and a host of similar issues. Where there is intense and animated debate on 'secularism' leading to unsettling social conditions, police cannot remain, in the 'ivory tower' or the isolated cell, but prepare their organization to operate under such conditions of conceptual cobwebs and diffused socio-political interpretations, so that they do not stand condemned or stereo-types such as a 'communalized' force. Police have to swim in polluted waters, but without getting polluted in the process. 'Naxalism' has emerged and continues to remain as an issue without a coherent and uniform understanding. Several states are affected and yet no two states seem to agree, at least explicitly, on the concept and mode of dealing with the 'problem'. There are several 'all-India' crimes and states demand financial and other support to meet the challenges to internal security. But, even at a time when demarcation between the external and the internal security has melted to make it a 'continuum', states seem to feel comfortable to stand in 'autonomous' isolation. In such situations the police have a professional role to articulate and help shape public opinion and policy. Public opinion and policy explorations become a part of the professional role of the police, to be undertaken on a research or on a think-tank mode. Agencies like the BPR & D have a critical role in shaping and pursuing TROD models and approaches.

The fourth aspect of the agenda encompasses issues emerging on the frontier areas. There is a tremendous pressure and process of modernization of police organizations – in terms of information and communication technology, mobility, upgradation of equipment and weaponry, and enhancement of the skills of manpower. Yet the police forces are today at conflict with themselves on account of a hazy understanding of the concept, nature and extent of 'professionalization' of the police. It can be hypothesized that rapid modernization without matching professionalization can be counter-productive and dangerous to society as well as to the efficacy and image of the police. This gap was reflected upon by a senior police officer when he said: "We are professionals but working for unprofessional organizations." If it is so, how can one resolve such contradictory situations; and whose task is it to do so? There is a hazy understanding of a 'profession' and its attributes. It can be stated that it is due to the low-levels of professional ethos that the police in India have become an instrument of partisan politics with a disastrous impact on their own self-image and esteem, *espirit de corps*, standards of performance, and myriad manifestations of corruption. Viewed one way, thus, professionalization demands parity with, if not priority over, modernization. The professional slide is one of the important factors that has led to a devaluation of the civil/state police forces in India, and emergence of central police organizations (CPOs), para-military forces (PMFs) and deployment of armed forces on the domestic stage. There emerged clearly a hierarchy among the police organizations, adversely affecting the process of complementarity. There is perhaps room for exploring innovative initiatives such as designing (a) a 'social audit' mechanism, and (b) designing traffic management as a 'schooling for democracy'. The age old logic of increasing police manpower in proportion to rapid increases in population can be given up in favour of changing the character of the police force in the direction of enhancing its productivity. Police organizations (esp. the leadership) can explore ways of enhancing performance, transparency and credibility, so as to build a positive image and relationship with the community. Otherwise, (as one study reported) the self-image (and esteem) of the police that was found to be lower than the image of the police as held by the public, clouds the image as well as performance of the police.

Finally, the fifth aspect of the police agenda revolves around questions that arise and responses that are formulated. All police organizations have created research cells or units, but these are not yielding commensurate, applicable output. Empirical research has several pitfalls if not designed and pursued rigorously. The question as to how far the present popular perceptions that police is communalized, (or subjected to partisan politics), or criminalized, can be answered on the basis of empirical 'evidence'. In the absence of empirical evidence, prejudices reign supreme. Similarly another interesting question could be formulated around the issue of increased use of information and communication technology in the police organizations. The question is how and how far increased information and communication technology (ICT) has facilitated organizational decentralization and participation, or whether and how, it has contributed, unwittingly to the centralization of authority and the decision making process.

Training (T) 'in isolation' of R (Research) and OD (Organizational Development) can be counter-productive and could lead to increased levels of frustration among the participants. This is so because training promotes awareness and equips individual functionaries with skills and capabilities. But such enhanced capabilities are not integrated and utilized through on the job transfer of such skills, to the organization. This is vividly reflected in feedback and evaluation of training programmes. Without research back-up, training is commented upon as 'theoretical', or as not related to the ground realities and field problems. Unless the 'concepts' are related to the 'context', training sessions get reduced to an opportunity to 'acquire' fresh knowledge but not 'applicability' on the ground, back in the organization. Research provides this linkage between concepts and contexts. Training can also lead to increased levels of frustration, especially among the more serious and perceptive functionaries for they find that they cannot internalize the output from training into the organization. For those not exposed to training resist innovation and application. The leadership finds that the organization is not ready i.e., not 'prepared' to absorb fresh knowledge, skills and processes of management. Organization Development (OD) provides opportunities for backward and forward linkages to research and training activities respectively. In isolation, TROD activities are useful but not adequate to the promotion of organizational performance and levels of excellence.

What is 'democratization' for a society is 'humanization' for organizations working in and for a democracy. In quintessential terms, democratization and humanization place the 'demos' the people, at the centre of their thought, word and action. This phenomena can be viewed from three levels viz., (a) the policeman, (b) the police organization, and (c) the society. When it comes to the police (wo)man, the stellar qualities of an individual aspiring to join the police force, comprise of quintessentially human and humane attributes such as uprightness, honesty, truthfulness, law-abiding righteousness. These and similar attributes encompass all adjunct connotations such as earnestness, being fair and just, morality, virtuous and a high degree of concern for ethics; civility that includes good manners and courteousness, and being free of corruption. All police personnel are 'good' human beings to start with, at the points of joining the force. The SVPNPA has placed a fascinating piece of granite stone, uncut and unpolished with an inscription that says in sum and substance that the NPA sculpts and shapes a 'raw hand' into a fine policeman.

Individuals joining the police force operate together as an 'organization' – in a dynamic manner rather than in a static pattern frozen for all times. People are chosen on the basis of their aptitude, they are trained and retrained thro' attitudinal conditioning into the finest police (wo)men. Their convictions and commitment then can reach great altitudes.

We may have, or may not have a statutory State Security Commission, but what prevents the police organizations and leadership from having a Self-Regulatory Mechanism (SRM) that helps police establish and promote the highest standards of civility? Such a self regulatory process can make any statutory State Security Commission redundant. Within the police organization, the existing hiatus between the officers and constabulary can be reduced, if not eliminated, by fusing all levels within the same organizational ethic and culture.

Strategic Convergence

Issues of policing and security facing the nation are numerous, complex and challenging to address within the classical framework of policing as prevention and detection of crime, and maintenance of law and order. The structure of police force, which is highly centralized and organized on the pattern of command and control, with a constabulary constituting 85 per cent of the force, having no decision-making powers dilutes its efficacy and accountability, and is not suitable for the contemporary challenges of security management. Where the democratic political process, with its avowed objective of social transformation, itself has turned turbulent, it is the task of the democratic process to harmonize the multifaceted conflict arising from social inequalities and injustice. The police seems to be holding the baby born of illegitimate political interactions and institutional transactions.

The political system and the instrumentalities of state have corroded and to some extent turned malignant. In such a scenario of institutional atrophy, reforms including promotion of functional efficacy and productive performance on the part of the entire range of instrumentalities – the political, the legislative, the judicial and the executive—including some of the institutions of civil society constitute a single matrix, and a difficult environment for the police to be able to perform and deliver the results. These complementary institutions, tend to pass the blame to each other; every one of them finds it inconvenient to look at itself. Much of the unproductive, and counter-productive functioning of the criminal justice system is constantly blamed on the police. The police tend to take such blame unquestioningly and silently. Police (leadership) have to negotiate with the polity in deriving strength emerging from a shared vision of the society, and clearly defined mission. In order to be able to do that, police have to strengthen their own organizational network first, by working together.

In Chhattisgarh the creation of Special Police Officers (SPO), per se, has added to the conflict which was already intense between the police, Naxals and the cadres of *Salwa Judum* leading to a public interest litigation (PIL) before the Supreme Court, with a plea that creation of the posts of SPO was not an appropriate mode for creating employment. The State government's plea that the institution of SPOs was in vogue during the British regime has only led to a series and more serious questions. The highest court asked the State: "Are you saying that the petitioners are Maoists? That is exactly the problem. Don't divide the society into pro and anti Naxalite supporters." Paradoxically, the Counsel for the Union Government argued (during the year 2011) that the State has only 40 battalions as against the need for 70 battalions, and hence the need for armed SPOs. When one of the judges, Justice B. Sudarshan Reddy asked the Counsel for the Union Government whether any rules had been framed under the Police Act, the Counsel said: "No, the matter is pending before the Police Reforms Commission". Which Commission? When was it appointed and whether that honourable Commission had submitted any interim report, if the issue of SPOs was referred to it were the questions raised but could find no answers.

The need to improve coordination and cooptation between the police and the executive magistracy has been noted repeatedly by the various commissions and committees. Some joint programmes of training have been mounted. A review of the efficacy of such programmes will lead to actions needed beyond esoteric training programmes.

Are we as a nation deluding ourselves in the sphere of national security on the plea of being a federal polity? Are we ascribing and assigning larger than life role to the 'regional', sub-national political parties thus reducing 'national' policy into a 'notional' security policy? Have our police organizations explored on their own, the scope and rationale for participation of local communities, independent of Panchayati Raj Institutions, in maintaining peace and public order at the level of local communities? What independent or adjunct organizational status and structure could be suggested for such community participation in policing public order?

There appears to be a lack of fear of punishment among the anti-social and criminal elements. The Mallimath Committee recommendation is to have the prosecution wing headed by a DGP, under the Advocate General. There is another view that a retired judge could head such a prosecution wing. Considering the inter-state and transnational dimensions of terrorism and organized crime, there is a strong and informed public opinion to categorise such crimes covered under a federal law and thus a federal organization.

Civil police have always taken on the heaviest responsibility in the maintenance of national security. Today, the police is left holding the baby, yet, it is not able to take its due place in the strategic planning of national security. The strengths and weaknesses acquired by and ascribed to police have to be taken stock of by the police themselves as the agenda and action, before negotiating with the polity. Such an exercise constitutes only a preliminary step. No other organization has been subjected to a prolonged and deep study by the series of national, state and local level commissions and committees as the police. Yet their output has been consigned to the archives without any matching follow-up action. How can the police organizations take care of the challenges and threats to the society, while they themselves suffer from several limitations and deficiencies of organizational health? Police leadership has to recognize that the state leadership is responsible for the status of the health of police organizations. A nation concerned with grave threats to security has to formulate a detailed action plan to promote strategic, convergence and synergy. Policing has become too critical to be left to police alone, especially in the situation where the organizational leadership has not exerted adequate pressure on the polity.

The nature of public – police dispositions and demands of 'good policing' warrants an exercise deeper than just 'public–relations' week, Police Commemoration Day, or 'grievance redressal' of the public. A comprehensive and critical analyses would throw up deficiencies in public policy, and the concomitant of 'good governance' in a dynamic democracy.

Police should not assume that the polity wedded to rule of law would assign a clearly and neatly defined set of objectives/tasks 'exclusively' to the police. Any or every set of objectives is entrusted to a network of organizations. Creating or securing conditions of a measure of complementarity has to be cultivated and operationalized as an exercise in convergence and synergy. Individual organizational design deficiencies or inadequate clarity over their roles and goals, characterized by historical hang-overs will tend to generate setbacks to the complementarity of roles and commonality of objectives. Police cannot afford to be passive at the receiving end, with a measure of despondence. Police that includes all other security organizations have to promote such commonality of objectives and complementarity of roles among themselves as a prerequisite before they attempt such synergies with other complementary institutions.

That there is a dire need to attain a high level of integration and institutional convergence in intelligence gathering and sharing has been reiterated in a report entitled, "A case for intelligence reform in India" brought out by the Institute of Defence Studies and Analyses (IDSA) funded by the Ministry of Defence, Government of India. The Report has advocated providing the various agencies a legal framework for their existence and operations, and a single authority for the supervision of its operations.

"A turf battle between M.K. Narayanan, the then Chairman, NSA and the Home Minister P. Chidambaram over which of them has primary intelligence and counter-terrorism responsibilities" is the reason for Narayanan's departure observes Digvijay Singh. Digvijay Singh also maintained that while the Intelligence Bureau (IB), the Research and Analyses Wing (RAW) and Central Bureau of Investigation (BI) all reported to Narayanan (himself a former Chief of the IB), "Chidambaram was bent on consolidating all intelligence, internal security and counter-terrorism functions in a single entity that reported to him".[50] Institutional dysfunctionality especially at the apex levels leads to more of it. In the highly politicized ambience today, there is hardly any room for professionals to display any sign of independence and professionalism in managing organizations.

In the sphere of the criminal justice system, the Judiciary shows its exasperation over the fact of mounting numbers of under trials locked up in jails for years – pending investigations and trial. In this regard too, the police are at the receiving end. They seem to be accepting or silently suffering the blame. Their organizational weaknesses prompt them to shy away from a reasoned 'negotiation' and a holistic reform of the criminal justice system.

All the dialogue and partisan debate over POTA legislation did not lead to any consensus over a federal law for a long decade but the law enacted in a hurry, with a strange unanimity over the National Investigation Agency Act 2009, within a month of the November 2008 terrorist attacks in Mumbai, without (a) any serious debate in the Parliament, (b) consideration of valuable suggestions made on the floor of the houses; and (c) constitutional validity in the context of Indian federalism. Federalism is not a fire-wall, especially in the context of a threat to national security and integrity. One of the Home Ministers was reported to have expressed that in the Indian federation, there does not exist a "federal crime". Paradoxically, the union government mulled over the idea of transferring certain terror cases linked to Hindutwa groups, such as the Malegaon case and the Mecca Masjid case that were being investigated by the CBI. Whether such cases were transferred is immaterial, for the emergency emergence of NIA had *ipso facto* downgraded the CBI in the pantheon of police organizations.

Autonomy and accountability of organizations have to be meshed into a process of cooptation, almost like a fusion of souls. It is a function of the creative and committed leadership of the polity. Exerting pressure on the polity is the professional responsibility of the police leadership.

The conditions under which police have to perform and achieve results are not without contradictions. For those who develop a vested interest in radicalizing sections of society, moderation and liberalization are passports to political oblivion. Police have to explore and secure for themselves to take on the political system in restoring its legitimate role of harmonizing rather than generating conflict as their dominant ethos.

Police had successfully demonstrated their muscle in the process of maintaining social order in many a democratic society.

Conflicts are not inevitable, and it is possible as well as essential to resolve them as and when they emerge. We are aggravating our problems, exasperating ourselves, and neutralizing our national energies in fault-finding, apportioning the blame, arriving at unacceptable judgments, allowing the conflicts to grow to points of strife and turmoil on various facets of social transformation. The institutions and processes of conflict resolution are atrophied and are themselves trapped in the maelstrom of conflict. Have we created the impression, by our collective behaviour, that in India there is an inevitability of conflict and that it is the only mode of social change, or chaos?

Can we elaborate normatively and clarify what differentiates adequate 'force' and 'excessive' force on the part of the police instead of exposing the police to the trauma of *post mortem* commissions of inquiry?

How do police organizations deal with allegations and evidence or popular perceptions, such as (a) police are the principal violators of the law, (b) police are in collusion with anti-social elements, (c) police are corrupt, rude, use abusive language, resort to third degree methods and torture. It is interesting and insightful to note that the officers belonging to 31st (1978) batch of the National Police Academy deliberating over the future of the Indian police, observed that an analytical appreciation of the existing scenario became imperative in order to evolve a vision 2010 thus:

> "The Indian Police will be a highly skilled, professionally competent and equipped body of personnel, fully committed to safeguarding the lives and properties of citizens, upholding the rule of law and preserving public peace. The Police shall be gender-sensitive, child-friendly and sympathetic to the weaker sections of society. There will be total transparency and accountability in their functioning. Every police person will uphold the values of integrity, honesty and compassion. Police leaders will strive to foster a progressive, proactive and innovative mind among all ranks, encourage them to realize their potential to the fullest and pursue the path of excellence. Police persons will enjoy a healthy work environment. They will command dignity, respect and trust of the citizens."

It would be interesting to note if any subsequent reunion meeting reviewed this 'vision of the police, 2010'.

Creative Leadership

An overview of over six decades of experience suggests that the police have not overcome the drag-factors of the colonial legislative framework and organizational culture, much less attuned themselves to the realities of a democratic polity. If anything, the situation seems to have worsened, primarily because of hesitant police leadership in the face of a partisan political process. The police had been assigned a dynamic role, while police organizations remained static – with their antiquated structures, systems, leadership styles, organizational culture and values and attitudes of a bygone era.

The Constitution of India represents a blueprint for social engineering whereby the twin tasks of: (a) promoting social transformation, and (b) sustaining democratic governance are assigned to the police. As the society gets transformed, the instrumentalities, including police organizations, have to continuously get attuned to such social transformation, maintaining a dynamic equilibrium with, and within, the society.

The police have amplified their role, accepting whatever additional tasks were assigned, often due to manoeuvers by organizations more appropriately placed to perform them. As the levels of efficacy and morale of the police force declined due to increased role and load, their equations with the other sub-systems of the polity viz., political, administrative, judicial, media and of civil society had suffered a setback and distortions. The crucial factor that contributed to and accentuated the atrophy of police organizations had been their growth in size *per se*, and proliferation of a number of organizations, leading to the emergence of a self-defeating hierarchy within as well as among the various security forces. As and when a police force was found inadequate to the role assigned, instead of improving efficacy and performance, a new organization has been created for a variety of reasons. It was not their specialization, but proliferation that damaged the image, efficacy and morale of the police in India. Police are aware of this self-inflicted damage to their image and morale. They are aware this damage and the consequent loss of esteem in the eyes of the public.

The Central Reserve Police Force (CRPF) is the most mobile force by design, and is deployed in a wide range of internal security situations. It is observed empirically, that the levels of their morale and motivation are high, on account of the bond between the leaders and the constabulary of the CRPF. If the CRPF continues to be a force to reckon with, it is the quality of its leadership and morale of the personnel, that emerge as the critical variables.

People who must be in the know of things say that squabbles among the top echelons of police seemed to have cast their shadows on the force when Maoists were making determined efforts to stage a return. In the face of disastrous performance in specific situations, the entire organization gets the blame. Credit for credible and creditable performance is appropriated by the political and police leaders, while shortcomings and failure are blamed on the juniors.

If autonomy and accountability of the police are considered a *sine qua non* for sustaining parliamentary democracy in India, the leadership (of all sectors including the police) have to don their thinking caps all the time as a constant, and put to test, their creative talents in promoting the structural integration and organizational synergy.

Police in India have made significant strides in technological advances, in aspects such as computerization, tele-communications, etc. But, the observations of the Police Commission of 1902, appointed by Lord Curzon, continue to dog the police in India even today: "The police are generally regarded as corrupt and have utterly failed to gain the confidence and cooperation of the people", not only holds good even in the 21st century democracy, but how that the situation has degenerated vastly. "Before independence the police were regarded as agents of oppression. Since independence, they are free of this stigma but remain objects of considerable hostility as officials who can be bought and sold and who mistreat the poor while allowing the rich to go free."[51]

A non-professional and generalist approach on the part of the political and bureaucratic leadership, with some rare exceptions, has led to an 'experience' based approach to problems of security. This was illustrated, glaringly, in one instance in the wake of the Babri Masjid demolition in Ayodhya. When the Prime Minister (PM) convened a meeting of all the concerned secretaries for a review, at the very start, when the PM asked as to how many of them had visited Ayodhya, it was revealed that none had. The meeting was adjourned with a direct that they should first visit Ayodhya. They flew together in a special aircraft to have that first-hand understanding.

An occasional statement, (or outburst, in moments of frustration!?) the Chief of a State Police force might speak out that the State Government tied the hands of the police from cracking down on the (oil) mafia which goes to the extent of murdering the Nasik Additional Collector on the strength of political 'support' which almost always is rooted in cash or kind, if not both. The political leadership keep doing, silently, what they want, in their pursuit of power and pelf. The professional leaders explain away or conceal vital facts, in a very defensive manner, covering their own weaknesses and limitations. Potter Steward's observations are very instructional: "The hallmark of a truly effective security system would be the maximum possible disclosure, recognizing that secrecy can best be preserved only when credibility is truly maintained."[52]

In the sphere of security management, in particular, a general comprehensive appreciation of the problem is not 'shared' as between the politicians, the generalist bureaucracy and the police leadership. If the political leadership looks at problems such as communalism, naxalism and extremism through the prism of partisan political process, the generalist bureaucracy demonstrates an attitudinal disposition of "know all". It was Rajiv Gandhi who had tried, for the first time in India to impart a measure of 'specialization' to the generalist bureaucracy by organizing them into groups, specializing in clusters of policy issues, such as agriculture and rural development, industry, economic affairs, social welfare et al. Rajiv Gandhi had initiated a series of management appreciation and development programmes to the generalist bureaucrats. Unfortunately, one term as Prime Minister proved too short to consolidate such an initiative, especially in the year 'reform-resistant' characteristic of Indian bureaucracy. In a review of one of the (four-week training and) development programmes taken up by Rajiv Gandhi, as the PM, one of the participants of the level of a Joint-Secretary at the Centre had observed: "Sir, one week duration was enough for such programmes as our absence for four-weeks results in our work piling up." The PM had shot back: "What happens to the pendency of your work when you go to Harvard or Oxford for programmes of nine-months duration?"

Contrary to popular perceptions, and to the bureaucratic disposition, in a series of national workshops organized exclusively for Ministers from different States (administered by such diverse range of political parties as the Akali Dal, Janata Dal, Indian National Congress, Bharatiya Janata Party, CPI(M) Telugu Desam; AIDMK, DMK, NCP et al.) the participating Ministers proved to be highly disciplined, receptive, and seeking optional sessions on specific problems like: (a) left wing extremism, (b) Minister–Civil Servants role-relationship, (c) preparation and analysis of annual financial budgets, etc. The interactions across party lines have been most creative and absorbing. Though these interactions demonstrate the positive attribute or disposition to 'learn', it is deplorable that there are no institutionalized opportunities for such interactions among political leaders across party lines. It may be a political deficiency, but it is an aberration of democratic governance in public policy formulation and management. Such deficiencies not merely reflect on leadership but more critically on organizations.

In the era of coalition politics where about a dozen parties, many of them based on language, caste, communal and regional 'local' agenda, the compulsions of their 'coalition *Dharma*' tilts them towards 'power'. Vital issues such as 'national' security become 'notional'. Even parliamentary and legislative committees, where it is expected that public affairs would be discussed with a sense of concern, are excluded from the 'coalition *Karma*'.

It was a refreshing change to hear from the Director General of Police, Maharashtra state Ajit Parasnis, that "We don't talk about our intelligence inputs publicly. No comments," in the background of reported buying of 17 tickets for the terrorist group based in Bangladesh for the World Cup Final in Mumbai on the 2 April, 2011. Quite a contrast from the patriotic partisans of different hues who proclaim that terrorism has no nationality or religion, and go yet beyond strongly certifying whole religious groups as 'patriotic', and that no groups are operating from specific cities / places in India. Police leadership have to play their professional role in chiselling an approach as to how much confidentiality should be maintained in the interest of security, and what to share with the public and at what time, and to what extent. "Secrecy cannot be attributed to concern about national security. It arises out of callous indifference to national security and laziness to go through the original document and decide whether its release would in any way adversely affect our security."[52] "It is considered adequate if people are briefed when the need for it arises" .... Transparency is the best policy and strategy. Unfortunately, this is yet to be fully appreciated as is evident from the counterproductive government deletions in the Kargil report and the holding back of the appendices and annexures".[53]

The most significant and persistent image markers of police in India are extra-judicial killings, contrived encounters, custodial deaths, torture while in custody in order to secure evidence/ confessions, excessive use of force in combing operations, arbitrary arrests, illegal detentions, prolonged periods of detention without charge, harassment, detention of whistle blowers, and partisan dispositions in religious violence. It is the enduring perceptions of the public that shape organizational images and credibility.

Social mobilization is recognized as a vital prerequisite for intelligence effort and counter terrorism. Indian democracy has come to recognize the need for 'public cooperation. The leadership of all institutions lose no opportunity to appeal for public cooperation, but not many have recognized, much less attempted, to learn to cooperate with the public. If the police organizations are considered professional as they certainly are, then they must help educate people, and themselves should participate, in the arena of human rights. Each stakeholder group assumes a position of self-righteousness not often recognizing, but often betraying, the fact, that there is no exclusivity or exclusivism, but conflict, between the rights of different segments within groups, or between groups over the same right claimed by each. This conflict of rights leads to polarization and conflict in society. Police are caught in the cross-fire of rights even when they are not aligned in regard to such situations of conflicting rights. It is a creative challenge to the police leadership to maintain and promote an equilibrium and social integration while protecting the rights of all.

Police torture, in its various manifestations and diverse connotations creates conditions like the law of the jungle. Most often, police end up apologizing for doing the right things wrongly. From an entirely different angle, the police are commended by the public for doing the wrong things to meet the ends of 'popular justice'. Forced to increase convictions and punishment for the crimes committed, they cause unwittingly, loss of police image, credibility and efficacy. The Bhagalpur blindings illustrate the point. The victims in particular and some sections of the public appreciated the instant justice rendered by the police, although the judiciary and generally the public condemned the police for inflicting severe physical punishment (even in heinous crimes). No doubt the Hammurabi code of an 'eye for an eye' is no more acceptable anywhere in contemporary civilization, much less in the constitutional democracy of India, Contradictions which revolve round capital punishment, victimology and prison reform have to be engaged in by the police leadership, to educate the public while shaping the policy, law reform and police procedures.

Any 'thinking' organization, indeed every organization, has to undertake a measure of experimentation, for which the only guide is the code of ethics of such a profession. When such an ethical base is eroded for whatever reason, the public exerts pressure, especially in a democracy, on the polity to 'legislate' ethical standards. Ethics cease to be ethics. Truly professional groups dislike operating under a 'legal regime'. Hence, the need to look at, e.g. the Karnataka Zilla Parishads Act, 1983, as an opportunity to experiment instead of stonewalling the proposal *ab initio*.

Social audit of the 'performance' of (police) organizations is not a control mechanism, or an instrument of fault finding. It is a measure to establish direct equations with the public. It is one of the best available mechanisms to help people appraise police organizations. A functional and holistic appraisal helps secure support from the polity.

A variant of social audit would be the corporate style of public-private partnership (PPP), which is the 21st Century *Mantra* for evolving models of synergy. Community policing is an innovative model of PPP. Somehow, the police in India have not shown their innovative interest in this modeling, as perhaps they perceive it as an encroachment on the exclusivity of their power and authority.

There is a 'red alert' to the democratic way of life in India, where we need a 'rule of law abiding', and 'people-centric' police. Today, it can be stated that the red-alert is just not for society, but for the Indian police themselves. They must come out of this, Red Alert not merely to ensure their image restoration but also for the survival of democracy in India. It is a great opportunity given to the leadership of the police in India.

The Future Lies Here and Now

One of the critical challenges to national security is to think ahead today as to what is likely to happen tomorrow and prepare to meet the challenge squarely – it is like firing anti-ballistic missiles to destroy the enemy missile before it crosses the enemy territory across our borders. Such an approach demands futurological, holistic research encompassing the trans-national, national, political, social, economic, cultural and technological facets of national security. Such 'research' has to be meshed into policy orientations, training and development of personnel, and attune organizational change management, along with technological upgradation, all the time, ahead of the contemporary.

Does national security management constitute a specialist job? The answer should be explored, and seen in the context of the reality that the weaknesses of specialization emerge from its own strengths. In the world of interwoven destinies of national communities, security management calls for a holistic understanding and strategies, that transcend the 'boundaries' of society (characterized by alienation arising from the inter-play of the social communal, religious factors), trans-border transactions (crimes, terrorism, fundamentalism *et al.*), and technology (nuclear, chemical, biological). The 'ministerial' prerogatives, the generalist administration and administrators, the unsettled and unsettling federal equations of the polity operate as the critical variables of security management. *Ad hocism* is no match to the challenge of a coherent, interactive and integrated process of thought, dialogue and action. Whether police is a 'generalist' or a 'specialist' organization is for the 'ivory-tower' intellectuals to debate. Viewed in any manner, the police is an organization facing multifarious problems of society, on the ground.

The Golden Hawk and Black Kite described as two *Avataras* of micro aerial vehicles (MAVs), developed by the Aeronautical Development Establishment (ADE) are the ideal instruments that can be deployed during low-intensity conflicts and counter-terrorism actions. The Director of the ADE, P.S. Krishnan has stated that, "Soon, MAVs will increasingly be the eyes and ears of the nation's civil, para-military as well as military units, and will be needed in large numbers." Are the police ready to induct MAVs and other emerging technologies, in order to enhance their efficiency and effectiveness? The technological innovation and its potentially revolutionary impact have been further elaborated by P.S. Krishnan when he observed that, "We are working on versions that can sniff out or sense chemicals, gas leaks, explosives or nuclear, biological and chemical (NBC) threats. Though there has not been only financial crunch for the modernization of India's police forces, laxity in the ability and actual absorption of innovative technologies has been revealed, such as the impediments in the setting up of the Crime and Control Tracking Network System (CCTNS).

The apostle of peace, Mahatma Gandhi had stated that forgiveness adorned a soldier, but that only the strong can forgive. Such a strength cannot be derived from the lathi or the AK 47 in the hands of the police. It comes from the strength of character, preparedness and application of mind. Those who seek to derive and demonstrate such strength demonstrate the democratic ethic as much as the image of the police in a more enduring manner. Violence is better than cowardice, stated the apostle of peace, who lived a hundred years ahead of his times.

The recent nation-wide surge against corruption had demonstrated the all-pervasive popular experience and disposition towards corruption in all its manifestations to show that it only required a match-stick. It is not only black money, it is not only money laundering, it is not only about political resistance to police reform. Simply put, it is the debauching of institutions of governance that has emerged as a grave threat to Indian democracy and national security.

During the 21st century, what humans make of today determines the shape of tomorrow. Human actions determine the future of humanity at large. Until now it was the law of nature that had determined civilizational trends, shaping the life of humanity. Humans had started shaping 'nature', through their material and non-material culture, with three sets of 'building' blocks viz., (a) values (ideology) (b) socio-economic models, and (c) scientific and technological innovation, and explosion. Humans prided themselves in that they represented the finale and evolution from the big-bang, through the various species and life-forms to the *Homo Sapiens*, they thought they had 'arrived'. They had taken over the evolutionary process, through manipulation, and 'mastery' over the five elements (water, earth, air, fire and sky); caused the extinction of so many species and life forms, and entered into the era of Gross Social Strife in human society, which can be aggregated, neither under-estimated nor overemphasized in the form of two options between 'co-extinction' or 'co-existence'. The options are not a matter of intellectual speculation, but real; humans face them here and now. The frontiers of national security have transcended the territorial, and encompassed water security, environmental security. In one word it has encompasses all the five elements of nature.

The job of the police is not merely maintaining law and order, traffic management on the streets of Hyderabad and Delhi, and the like, but by doing all that they are trying to do, they are shaping the future of human society. Thus, by partaking the vision of a democratic India, they are shaping the vision of the future of humanity, as a part of India's potential role as a role-model, in shaping the global ethic for a global society. The sky is no more the limit, and space has no known limits or frontiers.

Annexure 1

Code of Behaviour for Police Officers, 1960

1. Neglect of Duty

No police officer without good and sufficient cause shall –

a) Neglect or omit to attend to or carry out with due promptitude and diligence anything which it is his duty as a member of a police force to attend to or carry out, or

b) Fail to work his beat in accordance with orders, or leave the place of duty to which he has been ordered, or having left his place of duty for a bonafide purpose fail to return thereto without undue delay, or

c) Be absent without leave from, or be late for, any duty, or

d) Fail properly to account for, or to make a prompt and true return of any money or property received by him in the course of his duty.

2. Disobedience to orders

No police officer shall, without good an sufficient cause, disobey or omit or neglect to carry out any lawful order, written or otherwise, or contravene any provision of the Police Regulations containing restrictions on the private lives of members of police force, or requiring him to notify the chief officer or police that he, or a relation included in his family, has a business interest in his jurisdiction within the meaning of those Regulations.

3. Discreditable conduct

No police officer shall act in any manner prejudicial to discipline or conduct himself in such a manner which is reasonably likely to bring discredit on the reputation of the police force or of the police services.

4. Misconduct towards a member of a police force

I. A police officer shall be deemed to have committed misconduct towards a member of a police force, if –
   a) his conduct towards another such member is oppressive or abusive, of
   b) he assaults or misbehaves with him.

II. No police officer shall, without good and sufficient cause, commit misconduct, as aforesaid.

5. Falsehood or prevarication

No police officer shall –

a) knowingly or through neglect make any false, misleading or inaccurate oral or written statement of entry in any record or document made, kept or required for police purposes, or
b) either willfully and without proper authority or through lack of due care destroy of mutilate an record or document made kept or required for police purposes,, or
c) without good and sufficient cause alter or erase or add to any entry in such a record or document, or
d) knowingly or through neglect make any false, misleading or inaccurate statement in connection with this appointment, to the police force.

6. Corrupt or improper practice

No police officer shall –

a) in his capacity as a member of the force and without the consent of the chief officer of police or the police authority, directly or indirectly solicit or accept any gratuity, present or subscription, or
b) place himself under a pecuniary obligation to any person in such a manner as might affect his properly carrying out his duties as a member of the force, or

c) improperly use, or attempt so to use, his position as a member of the force for his private advantage, or
d) in his capacity as a member of the force and without the consent of the chief officer of police, write, sign or give a testimonial of character or other recommendation with the object of obtaining employment for any person or of supporting an application for the grant of a license of any kind.

7. Abuse of authority

I. A police officer shall be deemed to have committed abused of authority if he –
   a) without good and sufficient cause makes an arrest, or
   b) uses any unnecessary violence towards any prisoner or other person with whom he may be brought into contact in the execution of his duty, or
   c) is uncivil to any member of the public.

II. No police shall commit abuse of authority as aforesaid.

8. Neglect of health

No police officer shall neglect his health or without good and sufficient reason neglect to carry out any instructions of a medical officer appointed by the police authority or, while absent from duty on account of sickness, commit any at or adopt any conduct calculated to retard his return to duty. It is essential and desirable that every officer takes special care to maintain and improve his health by proper exercises, etc.

9. Improper dress and untidiness

No police officer shall, without good and sufficient cause, while on duty, or while of duty but wearing uniform in a public place, be improperly dressed or be untidy in his appearance.

10. Drunkenness

No police officer shall be in a state of drunkenness which renders him unfit for duties which he is or will be required to perform or which he may reasonably foresee having to perform or which he may reasonably foresee having to perform.

11. Being an accessory to a disciplinary offence

No police officer shall be an accessory to a disciplinary offence either by convincing at it or knowingly be comic accessory to any offence against discipline.

12. Damaging the unity of the force

No police officer shall by commission or omission do or fail to do anything which creates or is likely to create divisions in the police force on grounds of religion caste or community or affect the reputation and effectiveness of the force as an unbiased and impartial agency.

13. Anti-national conduct

No police officer shall do anything which affects or is likely to affect the security and integrity of the nation or lowers or is likely to lower the repute of the country.

National Police Commission (NPC) set up by the Government of India in its report 1981 (Chapter XL PP 45-46) laid special stress on the fifth principle . . .

> "ABSOLUTELY IMPARTIAL AND COMPLETE INDEPENDENCE FROM EXTRANEOUS PRESSURES.

It also suggested a modification of the twelfth clause as:

> "The Police should recognize that their full utility to the people . . . is best ensured only by maintaining a high standard of discipline, faithful performance of duties . . . and absolute loyalty to the force . . .".

Notes and References

CHAPTER 1

1. Rao, GRS, *Constitution of India: Vision Reality and Reform*, CPPSD, Hyderabad 1998.
2. Jawaharlal Nehru, *The Constitution and the Constituent Assembly*, Lok Sabha Secretariat, New Delhi 1990, p. 34.
3. Granville Austin, *The Indian Constitution: Corner Stone of a Nation*, OUP, London 1972, PXIV.
4. Alladi Krishnaswami, Objectives Resolution, The Constitution and the Constituent Assembly, *ibid.,* p. 23.
5. Jawaharlal Nehru, Declaration of objectives. The Constitution and the Constituent Assembly, *ibid.,* p. 19.
6. Dr. B.R. Ambedkar, The Draft Constitution and the Constituent Assembly *ibid.,* p. 119.
7. M. Anantasayanam Iyengar, The salient features of the Constitution, Achievements of the Constituent Assembly, The Constitution and the Constituent Assembly, *ibid.*, p. 153-154.
8. M.C. Chagla, *Roses in December*, Bharatiya Vidya Bhavan, Mumbai, 1974, p. 81.
9. K.K. Virulkar, *The Soul of the Constitution, The Constitution and the Constituent Assembly*, Lok Sabha Secretariat, New Delhi, 1990.
10. For a detailed consideration of the issue refer G.R.S. Rao, '*Managing A Vision : Democracy, Development and Governance*, Gyan, New Delhi, 2005.
11. *Times of India*, Hyderabad, Sept., 2007, p. 9.
12. This historical declaration of India i.e. Bharat, has continued even after it attained political freedom in 1947. The Pakisthani infiltrators, supported and followed by its army aggressively occupied 78,000 sq. km. of Indian territory in Jammu and Kashmir. China has occupied in 1962, 37,550 sq. km. of Ladakh, with some more claims over parts of Arunachal Pradesh.

CHAPTER 2

13. Dr. Mahabub Ul Haq, Natinal Security : An overview, Vishwa Samwad Kendra, Mumbai, 2004.

14. Jeremy K. Brown (ed) Warfare in the 21st Century, H W Wilson, 2003.
15. The Hindu, Hyderabad, Mar 9, 2011, p. 1.
16. What Life Has Taught Me, Pitirim Sorokin Bharatiya Vidya Bhavan, Bombay, 1987 (3rd ed.), p. 39.
17. National Security Strategy of USA, Sept. 2002.
18. Brahma Chellani, Some Sticks yet more carrots for Pakisthan, The Hindu, Hyderabad, May 6, 2011. p. 12.
19. Shris Smith, The Diffusion of Small Arms and Light Weapons in Pakisthan and North India.
20. Girish Saxena, *The Hindu*, New Delhi, Feb 9, 1992.
21. *Sunday Times*, London, Aug 18, 1996.
22. Ranjan Roy, Times News Network. "Welcome to www of UN-Islamic Terror, *Times of India*, New Delhi, India.
23. *The Hindu*, Hyderabad.
24. For a detailed consensual statement on the problem, refer GRS Rao (ed) "Naxalism : Distortions of Development" RIIPAA Hyderabad 1991.
25. Convenor, National Security Advisory Board: General G M Kariappa Memorial Lecture, National Defence College, New Delhi, 19_ _.

CHAPTER 3

26. Aagama Sastra, Brihaspati; Vishnu Purana, Kalidasa's writings, Acharya Chanakya had vividly described the boundaries of Bharat's landmass.
27. M.K. Narayanan as early as 1993, one time Director of the Intelligence Bureau, National Security Advisor 2004–2010 and Governor of West Bengal 2010.
28. G.R.S. Rao (ed.) *NAXALISM : Distortion of Development*, RIIPAA, Hyderabad, 1991.
29. Koteswar Rao alias Kishenji, Maoist Leader, *The Hindu*, Hyderabad 7 Nov, 2009, p. 1.
30. Dr. Manmohan Singh, Prime Minister of India, *The Hindu*, Hyderabad, 10 Nov 2009.
31. Sowmya Mishra DCP (Crimes), Cyberabad, AP, in *The Hindu*, Hyderabad 3 Jun 2005, p. 4.
32. D.C. Nath, *Intelligence Imperatives for India*, India First Foundation, New Delhi.
33. P. Chidambaram, *The Hindu*, Hyderabad, Jan 13, 2009, p. 16.
34. Administrative Reforms Commission, Veerappa Moiley, Government of India, MHA, New Delhi.
35. Police Reforms Commission, Justice D.N. Chowdhury, Guwahati, Assam, 19 _ _, p. ___.

CHAPTER 4

36. India, Planning Commission, Seventh Five Year Plan (1985–90) Vol. II, p. 328.

37. Prime Minister Dr. Manmohan Singh at the Chief Ministers' Conference, *The Hindu*, Hyderabad, Feb 8, 2010, p. 1.
38. Home Minister, P. Chidambaram at Chief Ministers' Conference, *The Hindu*, Hyderabad, Feb 8, 2010, p. 1.
39. Prime Minister Dr. Manmohan Singh at the Chief Ministers' Conference, *The Hindu*, Hyderabad, Feb 8, 2010, p. 1.
40. National Workshop on Public Policy Management for D.G., Addl. D.G., and I.G. level officers, Administrative Staff College of India, Hyderabad, 1999.
41. Air India Flight 182 Kanishka, Commission of Inquiry headed by a former Judge of the Canadian Supreme Court, John Major.
42. GRS Rao Working paper, National workshop on Internal Security Management, Administrative Staff College of India, Hyderabad, 1996.
43. National Human Rights Commission, GOI, Annual Report 1994-95, p.66.
44. *Ibid.*, p. 67.
45. *The Hindu*, Hyderabad, March 22, 2011, p. 13.
46. *The Hindu*, Hyderabad, March 22, 2011.
47. B.G. Rajeshwar, *Times News*, New York, *Times of India*, Hyderabad 16 Aug, 1983.
48. V.N. Raja, *Whither Criminal Justice Policy*, Sagar Publications, New Delhi, 1983.
49. The author of this publication was reminded of a top police officer who stated, while responding with a heavy heart to a farewell party on the day of retirement : "Let me go back to the society and adjust myself to life as a citizen".

CHAPTER 5

50. Digvijay Singh, Secretary General, All India Congress Committee and former Chief Minister of Madhya Pradesh, The Hindu, Hyderabad, March 16, 2011, p. 11.
51. George Thomas Kurien, India : in World Encyclopaedia of Police Service Forces and Conventional Systems, 2nd edition (ed) Thomas Gale 1989, p. 477.
52. Potter Steward, Pentagon Papers Opinion, 1971, TIME, Dec 13, 2010, p. 37.
53. *The Hindu*, Hyderabad, 29.08.2012, p. 20.

ANNEXURE 1

54. Code of Behaviour for Police Officers, Formulated and adopted at the Conference of IGs of Police 1960.

Index